COMMUNITY OF SOUND

BEACON PRESS / BOSTON

COMMUNITY OF SOUND

Boston Symphony and Its World of Players

LOUIS SNYDER   Photographs by Milton Feinberg

Grateful acknowledgment is made to the following: The estate of M. A. DeWolfe Howe for permission to reprint the quotes from *The Boston Symphony Orchestra 1881–1931* by M. A. DeWolfe Howe which appear on pages 6, 7, 8, 9, 10, 11, 12, 15–16, 19, 71, 81, 85, 107, and 155; and *The Christian Science Monitor* for permission to quote from "Battle Music at Bunker Hill?" by Louis Snyder, July 2, 1971, and "Beethoven Battles the Elements" by Louis Snyder, July 31, 1974. Copyright © 1971, 1974 The Christian Science Publishing Society. All Rights Reserved.

Copyright © 1979 by Louis Snyder
Photographs copyright © 1979 by Milton Feinberg
Beacon Press books are published under the auspices of the Unitarian Universalist Association
Published simultaneously in Canada by Fitzhenry & Whiteside Limited, Toronto
All rights reserved
Printed in the United States of America

(hardcover) 9 8 7 6 5 4 3 2 1

Library of Congress Cataloging in Publication Data

Snyder, Louis.
  Community of sound.
  Bibliography: p.
  Includes index.
  1. Boston Symphony Orchestra. I. Title.
ML200.8.B72S946   785'.06'274461   78–53657
ISBN 0–8070–6650–8

Contents

FOREWORD   ix
I   JOINING THE ORCHESTRA—THEN AND NOW   1

II   AMONG THE CHOSEN ONES   27
    A Selection of Regulars   28
    The "Orphans"   42
    The Principals   47

III   THE ORCHESTRA IN ACTION   60
    Life at Symphony Hall   60
    Evening at Pops   78
    Off Season with the Principals   81
    Out in the Open Air   82
    Music along the Charles   87
    Radio, Television, and Records   89
    The Players and Management   94

IV   MUSIC AWAY FROM HOME   103

V   THE PLAYERS OFFSTAGE   129

AFTERWORD 154

NOTES 156

BIBLIOGRAPHY 158

INDEX 161

To all the players of the
Boston Symphony Orchestra—
past, present, and future

Foreword

> All the world's a stage,
> And all the men and women merely players:
> They have their exits and their entrances;
> And one man in his time plays many parts . . .
> —Jaques, *As You Like It*, II, vii

"Merely players"?

When Shakespeare put into the mouth of a cynical courtier his seriocomic summation of mankind's Seven Ages, he was thinking, as all great playwrights do, of the universe in terms of theater. "Players" were his everyday colleagues, portraying with the embellishments of their art the progress from cradle to grave of less aware human fellows.

Unfortunately, Shakespeare didn't live to experience another world of players—the symphony orchestra—which began to assume the refined form we know today only late in the eighteenth century. These players were of a new breed, tapping another sense, through new technique and discipline. Increasingly, composers explored the tonal possibilities of this grouping of individualistic voices, of distinctive instrumental sounds, and blended them to express musical structures and emotional ideas never before imagined. Inevitably, the players of this burgeoning music perfected their skills as they learned to meet such new challenges.

Instrumentalists, once undertrained and underpaid, have risen in the world artistically, economically, and socially as evidenced by an intense competition for berths in all leading orchestras. Musicians no longer need to apologize for their choice of profession. In Boston, for instance, to be a member of the Boston Symphony Orchestra is to occupy a position of exclusivity once reserved for Cabots and Lowells.

This book proposes to tell something of the player's life in a major orchestra—the Boston Symphony—pleasures, trials, and ultimate rewards, an occupation quite unlike any other. A self-dedication miraculously reserved for a chosen few.

Today's musicians still have their exits and their entrances, and in their time play many parts—but "merely players"? Nevermore!

I
Joining the Orchestra— Then and Now

We are seated in a concert hall—perhaps Symphony Hall, Boston, or the Berlin Philharmonie, or the Bunka Kaikan in Tokyo—where an audience is gathering to hear the Boston Symphony Orchestra (BSO) play. For some, this may be the first time they have ever sat before this particular group of musicians or even been physically present at a symphonic concert. Others may have known the BSO from years of concertgoing, from watching its television performances, or hearing its radio broadcasts or recordings. Whatever the situation, as the instrumentalists come on stage to take their places, the pieces of an extraordinary personality puzzle take form in a way unfailingly intriguing for the observer.

Who are these people, so different in size, shape, and age, and how does it happen that they were chosen to become members of the BSO? The suave timpanist with ear to his drumheads; the tall blond lady leader of the second violins chatting with a jovial snow-thatched clarinetist; desks of string partners fiddling tricky and disparate passages, each oblivious of the other; a first trumpet of distinguished mien listening to the tale of a smiling younger colleague; harpists skimming lightly over the strings; an eerie blend of sound from bassoons and oboes; a serene tuba player, instrument on his knees, casually surveying the increasingly populating stage; the pillared line of double basses, each in the embrace of a distinctive, majestic individual. What would have made that particular person choose French horn, and how do the women with flute and piccolo, cello, viola, and violin find life in an elite, predominantly male community?

As the stage fills, the mood for speculation increases with each new arrival. Even though this or that musician momentarily catches the eye and the imagination, the whole picture seems at last to be falling into place. A violinist finds himself on a teetering chair, and almost instantly Alfred Robison, the stage manager, has arrived holding a stable replacement high above his head. Elbow-room adjustments are being worked out among the cellos, while percussionists arrange the traffic pattern their battery of instruments will require for split-second execution during the concert.

Finally everyone is in place, conversational asides have ceased, and a standing signal from concertmaster Joseph Silverstein brings an end to instrumental warming up. First oboe Ralph Gomberg sounds the "A" and his colleagues take it up to become a one-note body. When the concertmaster sits, the tuning stops abruptly. Once again the solemn, time-honored rite of the tuning has occurred before the appearance onstage of the conductor.

Seasoned concertgoers as well as newcomers often don't realize that this age-old preliminary ceremony represents more than a housekeeping detail anticipating the arrival of the maestro of the evening. For the assembly of musicians it is serious business indeed, so serious that its timing—"no earlier than three minutes after the (preconcert) five-minute call" for the musicians' presence onstage—is spelled out in the players' Trade Agreement with the Boston Symphony management. It is the traditionally all-important moment when this massive body of instrumentalists commits itself to be *one* under the baton of another *one*—the music director—who will (to use Charles Munch's word) "guide" them through the complexities as well as the simplicities of the concert's program. Therefore, when the conductor comes onto the platform to be greeted by the audience, he and his collective instrument know, from immemorial orchestral practice, that they are at least starting on an equal footing, embarking together musically in tune.

Discipline is a word with many meanings, some of them stringent and angry, others constructive and self-continent. The orchestral musician is inherently bound by discipline of the latter kind. The chosen instrument demands it—and exercise within its confines comes into being when the conductor first raises his baton at the start of a concert. Then the player becomes one of many, giving a unique part to the total performance which only the conductor can fully perceive. It is, in a sense, a selfless contribution made by each individual, along with colleagues beside, behind, and in front, in behalf of a mutually congenial sound—a true blend of many personal musical achievements for the sake of the ensemble.

This personal involvement for the benefit of the whole is the basic lesson an instrumentalist learns upon joining an orchestra as a professional. The aura of being a solo performer must defer to the cooperative experience of being one of many soloists in a community of sound. It is perhaps the most difficult adjustment faced by the conservatory virtuoso who wins a place in a major symphony. Suddenly the rules learned long ago no longer apply. One's own sound is no more important than any other person's—discipline must be strong enough to confine it to its allotted place in the overall scheme.

For many younger players this fact of orchestral life comes as a rude shock. The scholarly competition and the transient nature of the conservatory orchestra can never fully prepare the professional newcomer for the powerful sound that tradition and experience have built into a major symphonic body. "It took almost a whole season for me to get used to not hearing myself," violinist Ronan Lefkowitz declared.

It was alarming at first. In student orchestras I had always led or played louder than those around me. I was lost in a professional situation until I realized that what I did must depend on what everyone else was doing. That meant relying on my technique and paying close attention to the section leader and the conductor's beat. Now at last I've gotten the message. Finally I'm tuned in.

The appearance of youthful players in major American orchestras is a recently renewed phenomenon, attributable paradoxically to attrition among seasoned musicians and an increasing awareness of the need for democratic procedures in choosing members for existing vacancies.

The earliest symphonic organizations in the United States were assembled through the persistence of zealous conductors who sought "men of the ability required for a first-rank orchestra." These they engaged, either from a limited pool of émigré "professors" who lived in America and were endowed by nationality or experience with a tradition of orchestral performance, or from abroad, on the basis of personal friendship or musical reputation.

At that time, American conservatories were not turning out large numbers of aspirants for careers in music, since neither the opportunities nor the economics of the musician's life had enough to offer anyone other than the chance virtuoso. Playing in theater pit orchestras, in beer gardens, or in peripatetic brass bands more or less encompassed employment possibilities for average native-born instrumentalists. Otherwise they earned their principal livelihood in a wide variety of everyday nonmusical trades. It was not unusual to see the butcher or cobbler by day playing a trumpet or beating a drum on the park bandstand in a summer evening concert. To the foreign professors and aspiring amateurs was left the playing of Beethoven, Mozart, and Schubert.

Theodore Thomas, a titan among early symphonic conductors in the United States, encountered many problems when he was attempting to form what later became the Chicago Symphony. Formerly the head of his own traveling orchestra, and for twelve years (1879–1891) director of the New York Philharmonic Society, Thomas in his *A Musical Autobiography* describes his trials in 1891: "... as Chicago could not furnish our leading players, they had to be brought from other parts of the world. In many cases the men thus imported were unused to such a rigorous climate as that of Chicago, and were driven away again by sickness and had to be replaced."

The Boston Symphony, founded by Henry Lee Higginson in 1881, gave its first concert on October 22 in the Boston Music Hall (described in *King's Handbook* as "among the finest and the largest public halls in the world ... lighted by a line of hundreds of gasjets along the cornice") and was the fulfillment of a long gestated and carefully planned concept. Two symphonic bodies existed then in Boston—the Harvard Musical Association, which had resumed concerts after the Civil War and devoted itself to classical programs, under Carl Zerrahn's direction, and the Boston Philharmonic Orchestra, formed in 1872 in response to the demand for more modern music. Neither had the kind of financial backing or rehearsal potential that Higginson provided for the new Boston Symphony, although, in his opening announcement, the founder assured them that his orchestra would not interfere with any existing musical organization.

Prior to his public declaration, Higginson had put his ideas about the new orchestra in writing:

My original scheme was this, viz: To hire an orchestra of sixty men and a conductor, paying them all the year, reserving to myself the right to all their time needed for rehearsals and for concerts, and allowing them to give lessons when they had time; to give in Boston as many concerts of classical music as were wanted, and also to give at other times, and more especially in the summer, concerts of a lighter kind of music, in which should be included good dance-music; to do the same in neighboring towns and cities as far as is practicable....[1]

Higginson goes on to question "whether a first-rate orchestra will choose to play light music, or whether it can do so well," admitting that "such work is in a degree stultifying," but decides that "a good orchestra would need, during the winter season, to keep its hand in by playing only the better music, and could relax in summer, playing a different kind of thing." He specifies that he

should always wish to eschew vulgar music, i.e., such trash as is heard in the theatres, sentimental or sensational nonsense; and on the other side, I should wish to lighten the heavier programmes by good music, of a gayer nature. This abounds, is as classical and as high in an artistic sense, and is always charming.

In his prophetic credo, Higginson asked "that the soloists sing good music always" and advocated giving "any new singer or player one or two chances to appear for the first time, if the aspirant is good." As for the instrumentalists themselves, he believed they would "gladly come in, because this orchestra will be the chief concert-orchestra of this city, and because a fixed salary is agreeable." Its suggested composition at the beginning comprised twelve first and twelve second violins; ten violas; eight cellos; eight double basses and twenty more to include winds, brass, and timpani—a total of seventy. Musicians would receive three dollars for each rehearsal and six dollars per performance. Conductor and concertmaster were, of course, to be paid more.

While Higginson touched on other projects—a school for young musicians, a mixed chorus, and the question of musicians' pensions—he concluded by saying, "If this scheme seems too extensive, I will only add that it is a wish and not an intention..." Shortly thereafter, it proved to be an intention that took very concrete form.

On March 30, 1881, a plan for a permanent Boston Symphony Orchestra appeared in the Boston press, signed by H. L. Higginson, incorporating in shortened form most of the features enumerated in his private memorandum: twenty Saturday evening concerts in the Boston Music Hall between October and March, with a public rehearsal one afternoon each week; the orchestra to consist of "sixty selected musicians" (actually, seventy-two performed during the first season); reserved tickets for the series at ten dollars or five dollars, "according to position," single tickets at seventy-five cents or twenty-five cents for the concerts, and twenty-five cents unreserved for the public rehearsal. Mr. Georg Henschel was named conductor, and "Both as the condition and result of success the sympathy of the public is asked."

Only the conductor had not been named in Higginson's early personal draft for his project, and who he might be must have given the BSO's founder some concern. Carl Zerrahn, conductor of the Harvard Musical Association, and Bernhard Listemann and Louis Maas, who (with Zerrahn) had led Philharmonic concerts, were known quantities in Boston, and would hardly have altered the status quo if placed at the head of still another orchestra (Listemann did, however, serve as concertmaster of the BSO during its first four seasons). Furthermore, visits by Theodore Thomas and his traveling orchestra, and local podium appearances by such foreign celebrities as Anton Rubinstein, who had conducted a dazzling performance of his *Ocean* Symphony at Tremont Temple, had exposed Boston listeners to greater conducting talents than they possessed at home. It seemed inevitable that Higginson should look farther afield.

By a strange coincidence, however, Higginson did not have to resort to the many European connections he had made during his own youthful musical studies in Vienna. On March 3, 1881, Georg Henschel, a German-born baritone-pianist-composer-conductor, appeared at the final concert of the Harvard Musical Association's season to conduct his own *Concert* Overture. His success was as immediate as it was unexpected. Henschel recalled, "A few days after the concert, I had a letter from Major Higginson, asking me to meet him."

The few weeks between the March 3 concert and the Higginson press announcement were busy ones for the thirty-one-year-old Henschel. He had a first exploratory meeting with the founder in which he expressed interest in pursuing a career as a conductor, although his experience was limited; married his Boston pupil, soprano Lillian Bailey—the principal reason for his visit to the United States; and on his honeymoon in Washington, D.C., received and accepted Higginson's offer to become the Boston Symphony's first conductor and music director. For the first season, to prevent ill feeling, he was advised to engage only local players, and by mutual agreement, his own contract with the orchestra was to be for one year.

Following the announcement, Henschel and his bride embarked for a short trip to Europe where, at Higginson's request, he assembled a comprehensive library of classical and contemporary music for the orchestra. Upon his return to Boston, Henschel himself separated and catalogued the music he had acquired, marked the parts, and thus laid the foundation for the BSO's exceptional collection.

Despite inevitable opposition on the part of old-guard musicians, some snobbish hostility in the press, and the competition of the

Harvard Musical Association and the Boston Philharmonic, which between them presented forty-one concerts, the BSO's inaugural season was an unqualified success from the first. The public flocked to concerts and rehearsals alike, and battles were fought in print and in person between proponents of Henschel's conductorial flair and opponents of his limited podium experience. Ticket speculators, those hawklike harbingers of box office prosperity, made their appearance soon after season tickets went on sale, while Louis C. Elson, a Boston writer not averse to venomous satire, wrote of Henschel:

That gentleman will appear as pianist, composer, and conductor, and he has already appeared as a singer in the series. That is a good deal for a man to do. But he will do it all with satisfaction to the public, which seems to be entirely captivated by him. The only thing he cannot do is to appear as a string quartette, or sing duets with himself.

Such manifestations of public involvement with this new musical enterprise were variously attributed to "fashion" and a "vogue" in Boston. But, having taken firm root during its first season—a total of 83,359 persons attended the twenty concerts and twenty rehearsals—the orchestra began making plans for 1882–1883, and thereby provoked another minor tempest. In order to consolidate musical gains achieved by having a permanent body of instrumentalists play under one conductor, renewal of musicians' contracts for the second year specified that they would be expected to commit their services to the orchestra and its conductor exclusively four days a week ("except if wanted in your leisure hours by the Handel and Haydn Society, nor will you play for dancing"). Some of the more venerable players were not reengaged, and the Boston correspondent for *Music* magazine protested that "many of the musicians find that the new scale of compensation ranks them below others of the Orchestra whom they had never regarded as superiors."

The musical press, undoubtedly spurred on by old-guard professionals, wrote indignantly of the Higginson-Henschel plan to "make a corner" in orchestral players, and establish a "monopoly in music . . . an idea that could scarcely have emanated from any association except that of deluded wealth with arrant charlatanism," despite the general admission that such procedures "may make Mr. Henschel's musicians work with better effect under him."

Fortunately more reasonable minds came to the defense of the orchestra's new policy. A writer for the Boston *Advertiser* pointed out that the degree of excellence a permanent body of musicians might achieve would obviously depend on the dedication of everyone to a single purpose. This, the writer declared, could not be attained by those who "played all the night before at a ball" or performed "every alternate night under a different leader and with different associates." As for differences with regard to remuneration, it was stated that musicians were advised to talk over their cases individually with Mr. Higginson who "dealt with the musicians in the fairest and pleasantest way."

The storm subsided, public support for the new orchestra continued to grow as an increase to twenty-six programs in the second season indicated, and the symphonic concert series of the Harvard Musical Association and the Boston Philharmonic gradually faded from view. At the end of the 1883–1884 season, Henschel retired voluntarily as the BSO's music director to resume his singing career in Europe, and Wilhelm Gericke, a conductor at the Vienna State Opera, was engaged to succeed him.

Gericke arrived to take charge of an orchestra which was at least on its way to stability and had won wide local favor. He was, however, considerably more experienced as a conductor than his predecessor, which soon made itself evident in his businesslike manner of rehearsing. His ideas of repertory for a self-proclaimed "Symphony Orchestra," however, were more literal than those practiced during the first three seasons, when programs consisted of a classical first half, followed by lighter music after the intermission. Gericke persisted in his intention to play music of truly symphonic standard, and he later recalled that Higginson had been his staunch supporter against a first wave of complaints and criticism. So despite some grumbling in the orchestra about a new and sterner discipline, and restiveness among certain listeners caused by changes in the programmatic status quo, the BSO's second music director forged his way through his first year. Higginson wrote: "There was no limit to his patience, and no limit to the pains he took; and he taught those first violins to sing as violins sing in Vienna alone. It was he who gave to the Orchestra its excellent habits and ideals."

Since the first four seasons of the orchestra were at most six months long, there was an inevitable departure from Boston at their end by many of the musicians. This resulted in an annual search for replacements and a persistent variation in ensemble quality. Therefore, out of necessity, a longer period of employment evolved. Instrumentalists were offered not only post-season "Popular Concerts," later to be known as "Pops," but the first extensive tours beyond runouts (round trips within a day) to neighboring places. Thus, between them, Higginson and Gericke formulated an extension of the symphony schedule which enabled them to promise musicians eight or nine months of work a year on a contractual basis covering several years, assuring continuity among the membership and an opportunity to further build a viable organization.

In the summer of 1885, Gericke inaugurated a practice which was to cause controversy among native musicians for the next fifty-seven years—the importation of instrumentalists from abroad. During his first season, Gericke discovered quickly that many older members of the orchestra were unable to meet the demands of the more difficult symphonic programming he had instituted. Higginson thought these older players should be replaced so he commissioned Gericke to engage twenty younger players in Europe the following summer. Among them were Louis Svecenski, Emanuel Fiedler, Max Zach, and a new concertmaster, Franz Kneisel.

Repercussions followed:

When the second season with the new members began, I [Gericke] had hoped the fresh element would make my work easier, and heighten our success; but I was mistaken. I soon felt that all the twenty dismissed members, with their families, were like millstones round my neck. The remaining old members took the part of the dismissed ones, opposed me where they could, and put themselves into direct opposition; a great part of the audience, even some of the critics, were influenced for the same reason. I was not popular in the Orchestra, especially as they did not yet understand why I should ask for better playing and more exact work than had been done heretofore.

This, like some earlier crises, was to dissipate when word reached Boston from cities visited on the first post-season tour in 1886 of the acclaim accorded the orchestra for the quality and precision of its playing. However, despite the tremendous contributions made by these and later imported members to the orchestra and to the American musical scene in general, the seeds were sown for what was to become an increasing demand for the protection of the native-born musician, culminating eventually in the unionization of the Boston Symphony in 1942.

Nevertheless, engagement of players from abroad, predominantly German, continued during the regimes of Arthur Nikisch (1889–1893), Emil Paur (1893–1898), Gericke (who returned from 1898 to 1906), Karl Muck (1906–1908, 1912–1918), and Max Fiedler (1908–1912). World War I, however, saw the rise of anti-German sentiment and patriotic pressure which ultimately maneuvered the resignations in 1918 of Dr. Muck and almost two dozen BSO personnel thought to be "enemy aliens."

For Higginson, then eighty-four, a believer in the transcendent power of music, the turn of world events and the fierce nationalism it engendered seemed to foreshadow catastrophe for the orchestra he had envisioned and sustained. Before he died on November 14, 1919, Higginson had turned over the operation of the Boston Symphony to a corporate body of nine trustees, whose first charge was to rebuild its shattered musical structure.

After the war, France seemed the logical place to look for replacement musicians and a music director, although the brief period between Muck's internment as an enemy alien (March 25, 1918) and the fall opening of the symphony season left little time to find a major conductor not already committed elsewhere. Although he would not be available until November, Henri Rabaud, composer and first conductor at the Paris Opera, was appointed to the post, and Pierre Monteux, conductor of French repertoire at the Metropolitan Opera, was secured to reconstitute and lead the severely disorganized BSO pending Rabaud's arrival.

The interim term presented difficulties for Monteux. Replacing the "expelled" German musicians with inexperienced Americans and whatever players from France could be secured proved to be an arduous task. After Monteux had conducted the reconstituted BSO for only two weeks, a national influenza epidemic caused the city government to close all places of assembly in Boston. When the ban was lifted, Rabaud had arrived, and Monteux returned to the Metropolitan Opera.

At this transitional time, language was a great difficulty in rehearsal. Rabaud spoke French and Boaz Piller, bassoonist, translated for the remaining Germans and for the Americans who spoke only English.

After one BSO season, Rabaud accepted an invitation to head the French National Conservatory, and thus returned to Paris.

Now free of his opera commitments, Monteux accepted the offer to be Rabaud's successor the following fall. As he remembers:

I was full of pride in my new position as head of one of the oldest and finest orchestras in the United States. Little did I realize the years ahead were to be full of trouble and embarrassment for me, as well as for the trustees of that sacrosanct organization.[2]

One of the replacements from France, oboist Louis Speyer, who joined the orchestra in 1919 and remained a member until 1964, has written feelingly of his "new life" with the BSO and how it came about:

In 1918 a Military Band was formed in Paris, composed mostly of professional musicians, to be sent to the United States for a tour of three weeks during a Liberty Loan Drive, under the leadership of Gabriel Pares of the Republican Guard. I was chosen as first oboe and was very anxious to go and see America.

In my student days in Paris, I heard of an orchestra in Boston, U.S., playing only concerts, composed of the finest musicians from different countries, under great conductors. Why should students of the Paris Conservatory know of such an extraordinary orchestra, in 1904? ... It was the celebrated oboist, Georges Longy, from Boston, who listened to the class and talked to us. This is why we knew of the orchestra in Boston.... For us, future musicians, it was a dream to belong to one orchestra instead of the constant rush from one orchestra to another to earn a living.

We arrived in New York in May ... but the climax was in Boston, in June 1918. We played two concerts, one in Mechanics Building, the second in Symphony Hall (may I say a dream came true). After the concert I was offered the position to be assistant to Longy. My first rehearsal, under Henri Rabaud, was a great experience ... at that time the members of the orchestra were called "the gentlemen from Boston," they looked so serious and important. The sound was beautiful, could I say mature? ... It was like a great family, everyone enjoying the work and the pleasure it gave to the audience.

To complete my "Americanization," I signed another contract. I got married in 1919 to a native Bostonian and when my daughter and son were born, I felt like a true Bostonian and had a very happy life.

The French influence extended through the successive regimes (1919–1962) of Monteux, Serge Koussevitzky, and Charles Munch and even into the 1970s. Violinists Roger Shermont, Michel Sasson, and Max Winder, who came to the orchestra in 1950, 1959, and 1962, respectively, carried on the Paris tradition, as did violist Marc Jeanneret, who joined the BSO in 1977. In the words of former manager/executive director Thomas D. Perry, Jr., the "European-trained—largely Paris Conservatoire—gentlemen artists of great dignity and artistry ... gave the orchestra a large part of its patrician character and reputation."

Another nationalistic element was added after 1974 when four instrumentalists emigrated from Russia to become members of the orchestra: assistant concertmaster Emanuel Borok, violinists Vyacheslav Uritsky and Victor Yampolsky, and violist Michael Zaretsky.

Certainly, then, the first imported players gave vitality to the depleted BSO, but other discontents were growing within the orchestra. As early as 1889, the Musician's Protective Union had challenged the importation of the BSO's third music director, Arthur Nikisch, as a violation of the Contract Labor Law—an objection not sustained in court. And later, Higginson had gone on record with regard to his attitude about the orchestra as an autonomous rather than a unionized organization, documenting why he said there was "no need or use for the Union":

The Union specifies in a way the number of rehearsals, the pay for the musicians, the number of concerts, etc., and interferes with the engagement or dismissal of men. As I hold that all these points are important for the good of the Orchestra and must rest with me or with my conductor, I see no need or use for the Union. We pay more, ask entire control of the men, and see to it that they are well paid, have pensions, and also get outside work if possible; therefore the Union cannot benefit them. We can keep the Orchestra at its present level or even higher only by asking such work as our conductor thinks essential, and sometimes the rehearsals mount very high, even to thirteen. On no other terms can I go on and pay a large subsidy, and not control—all this for the sake of art.

In 1920, though, with Higginson gone, eighty BSO members asked for salary increases, based on the wage situation in other orchestras. Thirty of them joined the musicians' union, so that the question of unionization of the BSO was very much in the wind again. The trustees demurred on the grounds that they were not entrusted with subsidizing the orchestra. But this was not the end. A provocative incident—the refusal of concertmaster Fredric Fradkin to stand with his colleagues at the bidding of music director Pierre Monteux to acknowledge the audience's applause—had disruptive repercussions. Fradkin, a proponent of unionism, was immediately discharged for breach of contract, and forty-seven of his fellow protesters refused to play until he was reinstated. A preconcert Tuning Room plea the next evening by Judge F. P. Cabot, the trustees' president, reminding them of their public as well as contractual obligations, swayed eleven of the forty-seven, but when the concert began there were only fifty-six musicians onstage to play an improvised program. Thus, the first strike in BSO history reduced the personnel from a full complement of ninety-six to sixty-five faithfuls, and it became the overnight obligation of Monteux to recruit and incorporate enough capable instrumentalists to complete his first season.

Monteux described the foraging process necessary to fill the empty seats:

Once again it was my turn to rebuild the orchestra. Happily the musicians I had engaged after the war episode, many of them from the French *fanfare* or band that had toured America during the last period of the war . . . remained. I gave auditions day after day and recruited a few fine players from the various theatre and restaurant orchestras in Boston and New York. In those halcyon days for the musician, restaurants had very good ensembles playing for the diners. . . . Many had never played symphonic music. . . . This was a worrisome and unhappy time, as I went on tour with fifty-five musicians!... The public understood our embarrassment and we carried the whole predicament off with flying colors.[3]

Fortunately, Monteux's patience and his uncanny ear had once more worked unsparingly to restore artistic order.

Monteux's "Herculean labor" to prevent the complete destruction of the Boston Symphony became increasingly evident during his tenure (1919–1924) as music director by his progressive rebuilding of an orchestra, albeit still nonunion. Except for the concertmaster and the first trumpet, all of the first-desk players had remained. The strike had taken twenty violins and violas, and eleven players in other sections. Richard Burgin arrived in 1920 to begin a long career as concertmaster and assistant conductor, and twenty-five others stayed on until their retirement age. At the end of the "strike season" the BSO membership had risen to eighty-eight, and was subsequently increased. The reasons for its newborn quality are explained by Howe in his assessment of Monteux: "A false note from a single musician, even in a back stand, would not pass him. He was sparing with his reprimands but he knew exactly how well or how indifferently every musician was playing." Upon his departure in 1924, critic H.T.P. of the Boston *Transcript* labeled Monteux "the restorer, the sustainer, the broadener."[4]

Considering his generally acknowledged solution of an almost impossible situation for the orchestra, Monteux may be forgiven a hint of bitterness in his description of his last years as the BSO's music director:

I did not have long to enjoy the fruit of my efforts, however, because I was told it was the "policy" of the Boston Symphony to change conductors every five years. I was replaced by Serge Koussevitzky, a Russian, conducting orchestras at that time in London and Paris.

It is the custom here in the United States to make an intensive *réclame* for the forthcoming conductor in the last year of the incumbent. Perhaps this is necessary, but I do not think the trustees of orchestras realize how very embarrassing and grievous, not to say vexatious, this policy (when carried out in the efficient manner of American managers) can be to a sensitive musician. In my case, I felt deeply my last year in Boston as a sort of interim between the known and the unknown.

I was told by Judge Frederick P. Cabot, in a charming speech made at a reception in Symphony Hall just before the season's end, "This is not goodbye; you will come back to *your* orchestra many times." I left Boston... and did not return for twenty-six years! Strangely enough, the five-year policy existed no longer.[5]

With the advent of Serge Koussevitzky as music director in 1924, the union situation simmered but never exploded with equal force. There were union restrictions against union members playing with BSO musicians, an unenforced blacklisting of Symphony Hall, and strictures against BSO members seeking to join the union. BSO radio broadcasts continued with only a few interruptions from 1926 until 1938, by which time the American Federation of Musicians' contracts not only with broadcasting companies but with recording companies virtually brought to an end the Boston Symphony's longstanding exposure through these media.

As the only major American musical organization still outside the union, the BSO was slowly being brought to heel by the AFM's new president, James C. Petrillo, who had succeeded an aging and perhaps less concerned predecessor. The refusal by the union to permit certain famous member-soloists and conductors to perform with the nonunion BSO was an early indication of the new attitude, and although Koussevitzky himself realized the inevitability of the situation ("Vee must go vid dee life"), the orchestra's trustees, led by their president Ernest B. Dane, who was now making up a large portion of the deficit, were obdurate.

Undercover plans (involving Koussevitzky) to contract the orchestra under union conditions to record and broadcast for Columbia Recording Corporation and Columbia Broadcasting System came to naught, and even the covert wooing of Koussevitzky by the New York Philharmonic to succeed Toscanini as its music director in 1936 did nothing to resolve this continuing cold war. Koussevitzky, torn between his loyalty to the BSO along with his friendship for Dane and the BSO trustees, and an increasing conviction that unionization would not be destructive to the orchestra, was in a key position to effect some kind of resolution. Mr. Dane, however, died in 1942, without leaving any kind of financial assurance for the continuation of the BSO. As a result, Koussevitzky threatened to resign.

The trustees, faced on the one hand with the loss of recording income and the departure of their music director, and on the other by Petrillo's willingness to assuage their fears of artistic domination by the union, finally made the inevitable decision. In 1942, the Boston Symphony became unionized after a long period of resistance by its trustees who had feared loss of "the wide discretionary powers we have conferred on the conductor in selecting personnel and in matters of discipline." As a concession, the American Federation of Musicians effected an alteration of its bylaws to permit the BSO's music director to choose musicians from among union members anywhere in the country rather than solely from the local Boston union. The provision for payment for overtime rehearsals, a longtime thorn in the side of BSO musicians, was an added benefit, as was an additional fee for broadcasts performed under sponsorship. A union scale was also to be adhered to in the case of commercial recordings.

Unionization, of course, brought to an end the casual importation of players from abroad by the music director, who during European vacations would hear and sign up a promising new talent, or encounter an old friend and invite him to join the orchestra, sometimes without auditioning. Not that these were ever less than worthy choices, but as one veteran member observed, "It was always a surprise to discover a new face from out of nowhere appearing in the orchestra."

However, as Moses Smith points out in his biography of Koussevitzky, there had previously been extenuating circumstances, caused by the regulations of the musicians' union itself, in Koussey's choice of personnel, despite his good intentions toward the burgeoning field of gifted native instrumentalists. All musicians who joined the Boston Symphony were blacklisted and any union members who even auditioned were fined. The penalties imposed, however, did not deter many Americans from answering the orchestra's annual auditions calls. Furthermore, Koussevitzky had almost prophetically foreseen the embargo on foreign musicians that World War II was to effect by engaging Americans during the 1930s, so that there was no repetition of the chaos produced in the orchestra during the First World War.

Despite the orchestra's newly won union status in 1942, the procedure for engaging new members remained somewhat arbitrary. Charles Munch, who succeeded Koussevitzky as music director in 1949, adopted his predecessor's practice of hearing BSO aspirants with the concertmaster, the orchestra manager, and sometimes a few musicians randomly chosen from the membership. It was not until almost two decades later, during the regime of Erich Leinsdorf (1962–1969), principally through the agency of cellist Robert Ripley of the BSO's Players' Committee, that an "open auditions" procedure became part of the orchestra's Trade Agreement with BSO management.

Nowadays notices of auditions for new members are advertised by the BSO in musical union and trade publications, sent to major music schools, conservatories, and responsible teachers, to organizations with minority listings, as well as to previous applicants in the master file maintained by the personnel manager. Information is included about the chosen dates for auditions, the position open, and the general requirements sought. Age is not a consideration, and both sexes and all nationalities and colors are welcome. "All we're after is to find the very best," explains William Moyer, the BSO's personnel manager.

Applicants are asked for a one-page résumé, which gives a comprehensive account of the player's professional and personal life, including training, awards, and engagements. Recommendations, in the form of letters or press clippings, are not required. Upon receipt, applications are screened by the principal player of the section where the vacancy exists, and by other members of an audition advisory committee. Although no one is denied an audition, those whose lack of training or experience is implicit in their résumés are either mildly or strongly discouraged by a letter from the personnel manager, but ultimately will be heard if they persist. Thus, no one is unalterably turned away. The trip to the preliminary hearing is made at the applicant's own expense; those chosen to return as finalists on a separate day have their fares paid by the BSO.

One month before the audition period a list of specific selections they will be required to play is sent to applicants. Depending on the instruments, these are excerpts, solos, or fragments from the orchestral repertory, covering as comprehensive a sampling as possible of the player's facility, musicianship, and adaptability to style.

Response to open auditions is unpredictable. For one flute vacancy, of the ninety-four invited from two hundred applicants, seventy-five or eighty appeared. Only half of the fifty violinists who applied for one hearing actually came to audition. Explanations vary: conflicts in schedule, the expense of travel from far places, second thoughts about the rigors of auditioning. In any case, the field is wide open in the BSO's search for the best.

The auditions procedure has been calculated to be as equitable as possible. At preliminary auditions, applicants are assigned numbers by lot and are allowed warm-up time. In their turn, they are brought onstage at Symphony Hall by the personnel manager who indicates the order of the selections to be played. The contestant is asked not to speak in order that there be no possible clue to the judges as to his or her identity. The personnel manager then announces the contestant's number (but not name) to the Audition Committee, which is seated in the auditorium behind a wide curtain that does not permit performer or listener to see one another. The Audition Committee includes the principal player and a specified number of current members of the pertinent section. The usual total of twelve judges is filled, on a rotation basis, from members of other sections. Thus, the panel for a violin audition might consist of seven violinists, a violist, a cellist, a bassist, an oboist, and a trombonist.

At the actual audition, the listeners sit apart and are asked not to talk or "give facial or visual cues" to express their reaction to the performance of the hidden contestants, all of whom are allowed to play through the prescribed selections without interruption. Each judge has a clipboard and individual sheets for each numbered contestant, with spaces to write, where applicable, impressions of tone and its use, accuracy, technique/facility, intonation, rhythm, articulation/tonguing (brass and winds), dynamic range, staccato, legato (cantabile style), endurance, range, and knowledge of repertoire. Either a point-rating system or the listener's personal reaction are written down to help judges refresh their memories when all the contestants have been heard. Decisions are reached at each session by ballot, followed by discussion as to those who shall be asked to return for the finals. Judges are told that there is no predetermined number of finalists.

Finalists are notified that they have been chosen to reappear and, if brought back to Symphony Hall for finals on a separate day, are

(Top) *Bo Youp Hwang, Korean-born violinist who studied and performed in the United States before joining the BSO, cleans rosin from his strings after rehearsal.*

(Bottom) *Musicians who emigrated from the Soviet Union, and later became BSO members—assistant concertmaster Emanuel Borok (left), violist Michael Zaretsky, and violinist Vyacheslav Uritsky—wait for the orchestra tour train in Germany.*

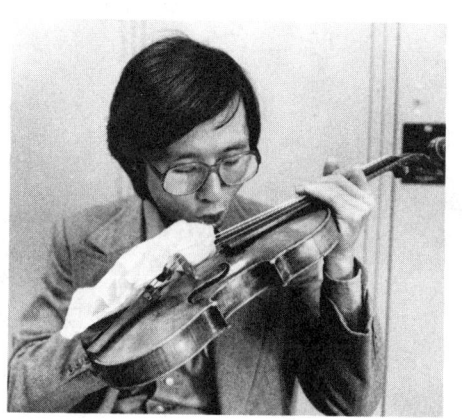

Carol Procter, marking her cello part during rehearsal, moved from the Berkshire Music Center into the orchestra in 1965 after a Tanglewood audition.

reimbursed their transporation by the orchestra. Now the procedure changes. Music director Seiji Ozawa joins the Audition Committee onstage, with curtain removed. Finalists are announced by name, and their résumés are given to the judges. Candidates play from the same list of selections as before, but more extensively—at least twenty minutes.

From ten or so, the field is narrowed to perhaps three. Each may then be asked to play with other BSO members to judge ensemble quality. The music director may conduct to test the player's adjustment to changes in tempo. Balloting follows each step, votes are tallied for each contestant, and open discussion takes place among members of the Audition Committee. The final decision with regard to the number-one choice, however, rests with the music director.

No one among the Boston Symphony's performing or organizational membership is entirely satisfied with the evolution of the open auditions. Some find it hampered on occasion by committee procedures, and others wonder if in the course of democratically intentioned competition a chance exceptional talent is lost. Among present BSO members there is a sense of empathy for "the suffering and frustration of those who don't make it," and while in this connection an orchestra spokesman agrees that "it sometimes seems to be a terrible process, there is nothing closer than what we're doing to achieve the highest possible quality. Given different committee members, the results of each audition might change, thanks to such matters as stylistic preference that determine individual choices. No decision can be absolute—so far, it's the best we can do."

Once chosen, the new BSO member is asked to have a physical examination by his own physician and signs a probationary one-year contract, calling for services equivalent to one subscription season and one Pops season. Thereafter, the instrumentalist's performance and personal record is reviewed by the music director and the Players' Committee for final acceptance. Then and only then is permanent membership in the BSO officially assured.

To the casual outsider, this may seem like a tortuous road to a berth, perhaps even a backseat, in a symphonic organization. However, it must be remembered that the audition represents a large investment by the orchestra in its future—the cost to the Corporation is estimated in the thousands of dollars to choose one new player—and for the artist it is a prized competitive chance at a major career achievement. (Though a rare occurrence, the process for the removal of a mistaken choice can last about sixteen months.)

After choices are made, contestants are usually reminded by the personnel manager that they should not feel "too desolate" (if not accepted) or "too overjoyed" (if successful), since many present BSO members were not engaged after their first audition—one young violinist played four times before succeeding—and for the number-one winner, the process of incorporating oneself into such a complex organization can prove difficult and frustrating.

The problems inherent in becoming a member of such an orchestra as the BSO decrease in proportion to the player's previous experience. Those who come from other symphonic bodies are apt to find the amenities impressive, and the atmosphere congenial on all fronts. Young musicians, particularly string players, have more difficult adjustments to make, once the switch in thinking is made from one's solo career ambitions to a place in a cooperative tonal community.

Cellist Carol Procter, a New England Conservatory graduate who joined the orchestra while still a Berkshire Music Center Fellow, observes that for the young player "working on an intensive level with intense people can be either a turn-on or boring, depending on how soon you learn to pace yourself in this situation. Once you realize that you're an adult, expected to do a job without games or embarrassment, you really appreciate what a good life it can be, especially if you keep up your technique—then you can do what you want with it."

"A wonderland of sound—this is it," was violinist Gerald Elias's reaction to joining the BSO in 1975, the same year he received Bachelor of Arts and Master of Music degrees from Yale University, after apprenticeship in the New Haven Symphony. A first conductor inspired him ("this is what it's like"), then a second ("this I wouldn't have expected!"). "We play better under great conductors and with the best soloists, but I appreciate most that the good musical instincts and practices of my colleagues in the section have rubbed off on me."

Although she had done "all kinds of free-lance work, from chamber music to jazz," before her engagement by the BSO in 1970, violinist Marylou Speaker found that she changed her playing in one year in the orchestra. "Playing speaks to the soul," she maintains, "and I'll leave the orchestra when I am no longer making progress in the direction of understanding, technical skill, and ability to communicate. As much as I enjoy being in the orchestra, I can't do without the self-challenge of some outside playing—recitals, or solo work with community groups. Being here hasn't limited my development."

As a nonperformer, Daniel R. Gustin, administrator of the Berkshire Music Center at Tanglewood and manager of the Boston Symphony Chamber Players, looks at instrumentalists objectively: "They're driven," he says, "and as much as I admire them, I can't say I envy them. It takes 20 percent guts, 20 percent exhibitionism, and 60 percent hard work, and if you truly have talent—a gift—nothing stops you. The satisfaction that an orchestral musician achieves can reach great peaks—one can really soar. But there are limitations too: technical problems with one's instrument can make a player lose perspective of what it's all about, and ironically, extreme concentration on performing technique takes its toll in terms of vision, of what music is. I love to listen, but I wouldn't want to sit in the middle of an orchestra for anything."

Fortunately there are countless numbers of instrumentalists who do want to occupy a chair, as prominent as possible, in the Boston Symphony and other leading American orchestras. Whereas in the early days, music directors had to comb the large cities for high-quality orchestral personnel, the last half century has seen tremendous growth of interest among American youth in performing—spurred on by an increasing emphasis on music in schools, by live concerts and recordings, and by a growing consciousness in the media of a latent demand for good music. All of this has created a buyer's market for talent in major symphonic organizations in the United States. The BSO, which employed seventy-two players during its first season in 1881–1882, had increased the number of its musicians by its fiftieth season (1930–1931) to an all-time high of 112—a figure not likely to be exceeded, both for artistic and economic reasons. To have the capability of becoming one of the 100, and to add that capability to the rich sound and tradition of the Boston Symphony, is a prevalent dream of players, not only in America, but in every corner of the world.

II

Among the Chosen Ones

The audition is over, and the end result, which from the beginning seemed inevitably favorable, now is in fact something of a surprise. No longer the aspirant, the instrumentalist is accepted into the bosom of a revered company of players, a select group known the world over for impeccable standards of performance. "I'm one of them. I'm proud," thinks the newest member, "but how did this ever happen to me?"

The answers are as wide-ranging as the birthplaces, the early lives, and the subsequent training of newcomers and veterans alike. For 100-plus musicians, all signs have pointed to Boston, from a clarinet in a dish closet in a sequestered Massachusetts town to a chance offer of a bassoon in a corner of Philadelphia. String players set their sights from Bulgaria and Hungary, and from right around the corner of Symphony Hall comes a hometown flutist or a violist. The rugged Northwest, for instance, can produce a piccolo virtuosa and a philosophic bassist; Washington, D.C., a girl pianist turned lady harpist; Minnesota, a burgeoning kid who dedicated his life to the trombone after first seeing one on TV. Who could predict it? Who can logically sort out the labyrinthine threads that brought these men and women onstage together to produce international harmony? Herewith a few pieces of the puzzle, some congruent, some anomalous.

A SELECTION OF REGULARS

In North Adams, Massachusetts, Pasquale Cardillo grew up in a household where his mother sang, and his father, who had played the clarinet in his native Italy, insisted on music lessons for his children. Perforce joining his sister in learning the basics of violin ("I hated the sound of it"), Patsy had his eye on his father's clarinet in the closet. Although his father eventually relented, he insisted that violin practice continue in addition to practice on the clarinet. However, when an accident to the fiddle made it unplayable, the aspiring clarinetist was told that practice time on his favored instrument should also be supplemented by that allotted to the discarded violin. "It paid off," Cardillo admits. "I loved to play," and with his father and a high school music director as teachers, he was soon the star of the school band and soloist in shows, women's club recitals, and other local functions. Meanwhile, he worked for the North Adams *Transcript* to earn money for further study and won a scholarship to the New England Conservatory. He also supplemented his monies for school with a loan from the family's musically minded parish priest. "The last mass I served as an altar boy was on the day I left for Boston," he recalls.

After four years at the Conservatory, Cardillo returned to North Adams and the *Transcript* with hopes of finding a job in a small orchestra somewhere. But an unexpected call from Boston asked him to become a stand-in during Boston Pops and eventually Tanglewood. The following fall (1939), he was invited to audition for the vacant chair, which he did along with a dozen or so other applicants. Previously he had acquired a handsome pipe in Boston for his father, whose acceptance of it was conditional: "I won't smoke it until you're in the BSO." After the audition finals took place, the Symphony manager took Cardillo aside: "Dr. Koussevitzky has asked me to invite you to join the orchestra," he announced with great formality. "It was the biggest thing that had ever happened to me," said Patsy. "I ran to the nearest pay phone and called North Adams: 'Dad, you can smoke that meerschaum pipe now,' I said, and he did."

Bassoonist Matthew Ruggiero tells, in his own words, how he first encountered the orchestra which was to be so much a part of his future:

My first contact with the Boston Symphony goes back many years when I was a preteen violin student in Philadelphia. I had just purchased a portable record player with money I had earned from an after-school job at the neighborhood drugstore. It had taken me all of two years to save up the full purchase price of thirty-five dollars. Mr. Castelli, the appliance dealer, must have sensed the magnitude of my purchase for he had thrown in a free record as part of the deal.

I raced home, tore off the wrapper, and read "Brahms—Symphony No. 4 in E minor; Boston Symphony Orchestra conducted by Serge Koussevitzky." Of course I had heard of Boston as being a city up north near Maine somewhere, but Serge Koussevitzky, I not only couldn't recognize, I couldn't even pronounce. It made no difference, however, as the wonderful music coming from the shiny new box on my kitchen table filled the room. There was a majesty to the sound of the orchestra, a richness difficult to describe with words. By the end of the week, I had played the record about two dozen more times. I was hooked! I had fallen in love with the symphony, the orchestra, and the conductor whose name I still couldn't pronounce.

A chance raising of his hand altered Ruggiero's career when he entered a vocational high school with a strong music department. There was a shortage of reed players, and when bassoon was mentioned, he volunteered. Since a neighbor was a bassoonist in the Philadelphia Orchestra, he had expert teaching immediately.

A closer contact with the Boston Symphony took place at Tanglewood as a bassoon student in the summer of 1951. I came in daily contact with people who had been just names on record jackets. Teachers and students from far away places shared my table at mealtimes. One could walk across the spacious lawns and hear foreign languages being spoken. I remember the new friends I made, the chamber music, the concerts I heard and played, and the scenic beauty of the Berkshires, all of which combined to make a thrilling and unforgettable summer for a young city boy. By the end of that summer, I had even learned how to pronounce Serge Koussevitzky's name.

After graduating from Curtis Institute, periods in the Army Field Band, a year of teaching at a Philadelphia settlement school, a summer at Marlboro, and three years with the National Symphony in Washington, Ruggiero was prepared to audition for an opening in the Boston Symphony for the 1961–1962 season.

Ruggiero recalls:

Never once through all these experiences did it occur to me that I would be an insider, a member of the orchestra itself, but in September of 1961, I took my place in the bassoon section at the first rehearsal of the orchestra's eighty-first season. Charles Munch strode onto the stage, and as his baton slashed the air, I once again heard the sound of Brahms coming from the Boston Symphony. This time it was the *Variations on a Theme by Haydn,* and this time I was part of it.

A Koussevitzky-BSO recording was also influential in directing the course of another musician's career. Bela Wurtzler was twenty-three and an estate superintendent in Hungary when his father, a prominent violinist and music director, urged him to study the double bass since only two accomplished players still remained in Budapest. Earlier, Bela had learned both violin and viola but without the intention of playing professionally. Now, however, the political climate did not bode well for one engaged in agriculture, particularly one who worked on a former nobleman's land, so he took his father's advice. He entered Franz Liszt Academy, and in less than a year had completed a two-and-a-half-year course. He became a member of the Budapest Philharmonic and of the orchestra of the State Opera. At the Opera, he met a baritone who, during a guest appearance in Vienna, had acquired some recordings not available in Hungary. Among them was one by Stokowski and the Philadelphia Orchestra, and one by Koussevitzky and the Boston Symphony. "This is the kind of orchestra I want to be a part of," Bela decided, and when he came to the United States in 1956, after the Hungarian uprising, he applied for a BSO audition (won that time by Leslie Martin). Accepted by the Detroit Symphony, under Paul Paray, after fulfilling an in-city residence requirement, he remained there as assistant principal bass for five years before joining the BSO in 1962. "It's the best in the world," he says, "an orchestra of virtuosos, any one of whom could be a concerto soloist. A group of fine people who get along with one another, unlike some orchestras."

More devious paths to their eventual goal have been the destiny of some, however. Talented, wide-eyed players on the other side of the world have not found the going as easy as it was for their ancestral counterparts who were heard by a vacationing conductor and summoned to an empty chair in a major American orchestra.

"It's harder to get into the Boston Symphony than to become President of the United States," said Bulgarian-born violinist Fredy Ostrovsky, who arrived here in 1940 after graduating with high honors from the State Academy of Music in Vienna. He came close to joining the Symphony in 1942, when, as a Berkshire Music Center Fellow, he played an eight-week season of festival concerts under Koussevitzky's direction. From Tanglewood, however, he went into the army and, while digging ditches in Louisiana as a member of the 95th Infantry Division, received word of his transfer to Glenn Miller's Strings With Wings unit in New Haven,

Connecticut. This unexpected turn of events had occurred, it seems, thanks to the suggestion of his Berkshire Music Center compatriot, cellist Robert Ripley, who had himself been recruited from an Air Force band in St. Petersburg and was being asked for names of top-rank string players in the service.

At the war's end, Ostrovsky spent the next six years (1946–1952) jobbing in New York and on the road—playing with the Little Orchestra, the ABC Radio Orchestra, and touring as concertmaster with Paul Whiteman's Orchestra—everything from classics to pops. An audition for Charles Munch was followed by a second—no decision ("a traumatic experience")—and then a call for a third. "This has got to be it," Ostrovsky decided. And it was. Now in his twenty-sixth year with the BSO, he feels he is "one person who is doing exactly what I should be doing, without gripes or frustrations."

Ostrovsky's Army benefactor, cellist Bob Ripley, had first been a Berkshire Music Center Fellow in 1941 after study at Curtis Institute with Felix Salmond. During the summer his playing had been favorably noticed by Koussevitzky, who recommended him to Arthur Rodzinski, conductor of the Cleveland Orchestra. Auditioning for a vacancy in that orchestra for the next season, Ripley, at age twenty, was accepted for his first orchestral job—at sixty-six dollars per week, for twenty-eight weeks. After a second season at Tanglewood, however, he was called into the service. Fortunately he was able to spend the duration of World War II in music, first briefly playing drums in an Air Force Band, then cello with Glenn Miller's active Strings With Wings unit. It was a busy assignment, both in the United States and abroad—weekly broadcasts, bond drives, often six shows a day, seven days a week, when "a quarter or a whole note was an event." But even so, there were scattered opportunities to play chamber music, and when the time came in 1946 to go back to the Cleveland Orchestra Ripley had a reasonable degree of confidence.

After seven years in Cleveland, the opportunity to audition for the Boston Symphony in 1953 seemed to be the fulfillment of a dream—Ripley had studied with Jean Bedetti, the BSO's first cellist. However, his joining the orchestra was postponed until 1955. Later he became a key representative of his colleagues in their negotiations with trustees and management.

Most BSO members attribute their choice of a career to interest and encouragement at home, either by parents who were performers themselves or had "an ear for music." However, violinists Raymond Sird and Ronald Knudsen are among the few first-generation musicians, and Charles Yancich declares that his mother and father opposed his playing the French horn. It would have been difficult for oboists Ralph Gomberg and Alfred Genovese to escape their calling, since both were raised in families in which brothers as well as parents were dedicated to performing. Concertmaster Joseph Silverstein's father was a violinist, his grandfather a violin maker; principal flutist Doriot Anthony Dwyer's mother had played in Ethel Leginska's professional All Woman Symphony; Darlene Gray's father was her violin teacher for twelve years; both the fathers of cellist Carol Procter and trumpeter Rolf Smedvig were composer-teachers and their mothers instrumentalists; violinist Ronan Lefkowitz's father is a musicologist; and two generations of music-lovers influenced Ronald Feldman to become a cellist.

Musicians in the family date back to Sheila Fiekowsky's grandparents, so it was no surprise when she began study of the violin at nine. By the age of sixteen she had appeared as soloist with her hometown orchestra, the Detroit Symphony, and had won the National Federation of Music Clubs Biennial Award. Study at music camp, the Curtis Institute, Yale University, and a summer at Marlboro were to have pronounced effects on her career. During the Vermont stay, the pianist in her trio was André-Michel Schub, winner of the 1974 Naumburg Award. In the Marlboro spirit, she remembers, "We had different ideas, but we worked them out." Later the two were married. "I had grown up in the same kind of family atmosphere as my husband," she remarks, "always compromise at home, no disagreements—together at mealtimes, whatever our playing schedules."

When she joined the orchestra in 1975, she became a colleague of two of her teachers, Ronald Knudsen, with whom she had studied in Detroit, and concertmaster Joseph Silverstein, who taught her at Yale. Life in the BSO called for adjustments—no longer was she expected to call her teachers "mister."

There were two grand pianos at home in Philadelphia where Ann Hobson was raised, and because her mother was a concert pianist and teacher, it was expected that she and her sister would learn to play under expert tutelage. From the age of six she practiced—"When I made a mistake, my mother would call out from the next room, 'No, F-*sharp*.' She had a very keen ear, but as time went on the feeling of competition became too much." Ann therefore became something of a rebel when, at Girls High School, she was given the choice of another instrument—flute, violin, or harp. Because of her experience with coordination of hands, the harp was the winner. Upon announcing at home that she had forsaken piano in favor of the harp, her parents reacted with shock. However, since the instrument was provided at school, it did not immediately pose a logistical household problem.

"I knew I loved it from the start," Ann declares, "and I didn't mind enduring those built-in problems for young performers—short fingernails and blistered fingers." With her enthusiasm and good instruction, progress was rapid. She joined the All-City Orchestra, graduated from Philadelphia Musical Academy and the Cleveland Institute of Music, where she was recruited to replace a player with an injured finger in the Pittsburgh Symphony. Meanwhile her parents' attitude had softened, and they became very proud ("as if this had been their idea") when she became principal harpist of the National Symphony in Washington. Auditioning in the second group of finalists for the BSO in 1969, she joined the orchestra as second harp at the end of the Leinsdorf regime.

Where and when one originally encounters the destined instrument is an ever-intriguing anecdote in players' stories. Radio broadcast concerts in the forties and fifties influenced Roland Small to become a professional musician. A native Canadian, he had spent nine years performing in Vancouver, British Columbia, before his BSO engagement in 1975 as bassoonist. Love at first sound was Norman Bolter's reaction at age five or thereabouts when he heard a trombone on TV's "Captain Kangaroo" show. The youngest member of the Boston Symphony when he joined it at twenty in 1975 ("I always seemed to be the youngest"), he survived being laughed at in school where instructors thought "it was too big for me." Finally, in fourth grade in St. Paul, an instrument was rented for him, with an extension added for his short arms. Studying first with his junior band director, and later with trombonists of the Minnesota Symphony when in high school, he persevered with the instrument he had persistently "bugged his family" to get for him. In response to a notice on the school bulletin board, he applied for the Boston University Institute program at Tanglewood, for which he was accepted. He was a high school senior when he spent the first of two summers there as a Berkshire Music Center Fellow.

Following high school, Norman went on to New England Conservatory to study with John Swallow, whose recordings had set an enviable standard for him. But, after a year, the plethora of free-lance opportunities—the Springfield Symphony, ballet and opera in Boston, and Boston Pops—persuaded him to leave school. Feeling that auditioning early helped him achieve ease, he found himself, at eighteen, in the finals for the post of first trombone with the San Francisco Symphony, and at nineteen, one of two chosen to be flown to Los Angeles for final choice as co-principal with the Los Angeles Philharmonic. There it was felt that an older, more experienced player would be more appropriate. Undaunted, he auditioned for a Boston Symphony first chair vacancy in 1975, and was chosen as second trombone the same year, when Ronald Barron moved up to the principal position.

Now settled in, Bolter has retained his basic enthusiasm: "I love so much to play, and to play so much," he says. "You can't be in a greater orchestra than this. It's a good job, with a sympathetic management, and a wonderful facility to play in." As a member of the Empire Brass Quintet, with BSO horn player David Ohanian and trumpeter Rolf Smedvig, he has toured Europe three times as well as the western United States, made recordings, joined Boston University's music faculty, and otherwise justified a youthful unwavering ambition. "Strings aren't often individually exposed," he remarked, "but when the trombone plays, everyone knows it. It was important for me to gain confidence at once—in a big hall, a big city, with a big audience. And it is important to learn to take it in stride."

Taking it in stride came naturally to violist Jerome Lipson, a third-generation Bostonian, to whom Symphony Hall was the shrine of "the one orchestra I wanted to play in." He attended Boston Latin School, where Leonard Bernstein was a classmate and his occasional accompanist, and studied with Georges Fourel, violist of the BSO. The existence in the city of a Young People's Orchestra, organized by Fabien Sevitzky, gave him some youthful symphonic experience (as it did to such later-to-be BSO colleagues

(Top) *Tuning her harp, Ann Hobson says of the instrument she chose, "I knew I loved it from the start."*

(Bottom) *A dream came true for cellist Robert Ripley when the BSO visited Amsterdam's revered Concertgebouw on a European tour.*

Concertmaster Joseph Silverstein and violinist Leonard Moss confer backstage during intermission.

as the late Reuben Green, Vincent Mauricci, Sheldon Rotenberg, and George Zazofsky) before he continued his musical education at the Curtis Institute.

At age nineteen, Lipson decided to engineer his own BSO audition. Knowing what he wanted and feeling very much at home, he took the occasion of a vacation from Curtis to walk through the stage door of Symphony Hall, instrument case in hand, and up the stairs to the conductor's room during a rehearsal break ("This couldn't happen now," he adds). There sat Dr. Koussevitzky alone. "Who are you?" he gasped, taken aback. "I'm a Boston boy and I play the viola. Will you listen to me?" Nonplussed, the maestro said, "But that's impossible. This is the middle of a rehearsal." Lipson countered, "I study in Philadelphia, with Louis Bailly [a member of the famed Flonzaley Quartet]." Storm clouds dissipated and Koussevitzky's face shone like the sun: "How is my old friend?" he asked. The end result, Lipson recalls, was a BSO engagement for Bailly, and a promise to hear his student during his next vacation. True to his word, the audition took place and Koussevitzky said, "Finish your schooling. You will play in the Boston Symphony."

Lipson served his apprenticeship in the Indianapolis Symphony from 1940 to 1942, spending the summers as a Berkshire Music Center Fellow. While at Tanglewood in 1942, the rationed war year, concerts were given by the Music Center Orchestra under Koussevitzky's direction for audiences who came "on foot, in hay wagons from the surrounding countryside, and by taxi from New York." Lipson went into the service in 1942, but his army career as a control tower operator was cut short when he was summoned to play in the orchestra for the widely toured Air Force show, "Winged Victory," and later with the Strings With Wings program under Tex Beneke's direction. Released from the service, he joined the BSO in 1946, thereafter becoming active for many years with the

Players' Committee in its contract negotiations with the Boston Symphony Corporation. "Mutual understanding produced agreements for the good of everyone," Lipson says with a certain pride. "The BSO contract and the overall job—Symphony Hall, the Pops, and Tanglewood—are the envy of all, a well-rounded existence. When the players from the Philadelphia Orchestra come from Saratoga to Tanglewood to play golf with us, they can't get over it. They say, 'What kind of a deal do you have anyway?'"

For many BSO instrumentalists, an encouraging first contact with the art and dignity of performing occurred in a school orchestra or band, often under the guidance of a music director prescient enough to spot an unusual talent and send it on its way. Such was the case with James Pappoutsakis. Born in Cairo, Egypt, of Greek parents, he came to the United States at an early age and grew up in Boston. Through the music education program at Boston Latin School, an older brother had learned to play the viola. When Jimmie reached high school age, he was urged to choose an instrument for himself. "What have you got?" he recalled asking, and when a flute was offered, he took to it from the start. "It was a natural instrument—I couldn't see anything difficult about it." His first lessons (at the then steep rate of from one dollar to two dollars an hour) were from Harry Moscovitz, a pupil of the BSO's Georges Laurent, and it was from this first teacher that he acquired his concept of tone. Soon Moscovitz suggested that Jimmie study with Laurent, the acknowledged virtuoso of the time in Boston, at New England Conservatory. This he did and upon graduation he was in demand as a free-lancer, playing in the WBZ radio orchestra, in trios at the old Hotel Touraine, and in the government-sponsored WPA Orchestra, which provided invaluable repertory training.

By chance, Pappoutsakis was heard by Bernard Zighéra, the BSO's harpist-pianist, at a chamber concert in the courtyard of the

Boston Public Library. Also by chance, Zighéra asked harpist Louise Came (later to become Mrs. Pappoutsakis) if she knew who the flutist was, and she directed him to Jimmie's apartment. "I was surprised when this stranger appeared one day at my door," Pappoutsakis remembered, "and asked me if I would like to audition for Dr. Koussevitzky. It was set for 9:00 A.M. on what turned out to be a rainy dark Monday, but Koussevitzky was there, and so was I. First I played the *Chaminade Concertino,* and the maestro nodded approval, then he asked the librarian to get Ravel's *Daphnis,* which was still rather a novelty in Boston in the thirties. 'But I *know* it,' I said and, to Koussey's astonishment, played it from memory. That did it. He offered me piccolo right away, or flute the next season. I took flute and joined the orchestra in 1937 as assistant to Laurent, my teacher. But our relationship changed. He treated me as a colleague, not as a student, and left criticisms and suggestions to the conductor, which was right. Laurent did not pull rank."

Inevitably, jazz and its related offspring have been influential in the technical development of many twentieth-century musicians. Increasingly, the BSO has been happy that within its midst are proficient players of many instruments not found on the traditional symphonic roster, like electric guitar, saxophone, or marimba. These instruments turn up in pieces by present-day writers for orchestra, as do rhythmic techniques, beloved of bassists, brassists, and percussionists, not generally associated with Symphony Hall.

Playing jazz supported Leslie Martin's symphonic inclinations during his early years in his native Seattle. Son of a musical family, his father, a singer, had given him a double bass at age ten, which, when he brought it to school, suddenly put him in demand for jazz groups and orchestras. Although he was kept busy in combos and later studying at the University of Washington, in 1937 he joined the Seattle Symphony, then under the direction of

Sir Thomas Beecham. In 1950, he came east for a summer at the Berkshire Music Center, where Koussevitzky was very impressed with his playing. "He showed me his own Amati bass," Martin recalls, "fed me all kinds of Russian delicacies, and suggested that I was ready to play principal in the Israel Philharmonic, but the next day at rehearsal, he ate me up!" Somewhat crestfallen, "Tiny" (a monumental man) was soon back playing jazz with the legendary likes of Ted Weems, Jan Garber, and Gene Krupa. But unwilling to discard thoughts of a career in a major orchestra, he auditioned for an opening in the BSO in 1956, during the Munch regime, and joined the orchestra a year later.

"The symphony is a discipline," Martin says. "I must adhere to the dictates of a composer and a conductor. My mind runs the full gamut of emotions ... but I am still restricted. I am but one of a hundred voices." On the other hand, "jazz represents freedom and exhilaration. I play it for fun and joy. It is a release, but I must still have discipline to be a complete musician."

Tiny has managed to have the best of both worlds. He is a symphony player, and also a member of WUZ, a quartet formed with three other jazz-loving BSO colleagues—percussionists Arthur Press and Thomas Gauger, and bass clarinetist Felix Viscuglia—who are similarly in search of that necessary contrast.

Like most young percussionists, both Press and Gauger found an outlet for their talents by playing popular music. However, Press became a student at the Juilliard School, later working with the Little Orchestra of New York and at Radio City Music Hall before joining the BSO in 1956. Gauger, reared in a family of musicians in Illinois, had been a member of the ensemble formed by the American instrumental innovator, Harry Partch, prior to becoming a member of the BSO's percussion section in 1963. For both of them, as for Martin, their membership in WUZ continues to provide a performing balance between symphonic and popular techniques.

Despite the difficulty of attaining a place in the Boston Symphony, there are occasionally those who do not choose to stay. Peter Gordon grew up in a musical family—his father was a violist-conductor, his mother a singer, and relatives included two stars of Toscanini's NBC Symphony, violinist Mischa Mischakoff and trumpeter Harry Glantz. Violin was his first instrument, and during his teens he played in the student orchestra at Chautauqua where his family spent numerous summers. With the army looming, he felt he should master a brass instrument, so he took it upon himself to learn the French horn, which he played during his high school years and later at Indiana University. An exchange program between the university and Brazil took him as a member of a woodwind quintet to a Latin American music festival in Brasilia, where one of his duties was to teach brass playing to the presidential guard. A political upheaval brought the festival to a sudden end. Returning home, he worked for one year each in the Toledo Symphony and the Philadelphia Chamber Orchestra. Following a period of free-lancing in New York, and chamber music engagements in such far-flung spots as Aegina, Greece, and Portland, Oregon, Peter joined the Metropolitan Opera Orchestra from 1970 to 1973, subsequently playing jazz with several bands to help satisfy his interest in improvisation. "I always was looking for a place to sit-in," he says. When a second horn opening occurred in the BSO, he was urged to audition. As a result, he was offered the job, joining the orchestra at Tanglewood in the summer of 1976—a contrast to his earlier membership in the rock group Blood, Sweat, and Tears. But his personal interest in the French horn ("not a popular instrument but still an outlet for music") and his search for ways to "expand its perimeters, coupled with a feeling of constriction in the fabric of a large symphonic body," brought about his decision to leave the orchestra after the summer of 1978. "I learned a lot at the BSO," he declares, "but I felt I was losing my fine edge, and in a free-lance situation, playing all kinds of music, I'd have more opportunities to fulfill myself and maintain a kind of spiritual security."

For Felix Viscuglia, bass clarinetist with the orchestra for twelve years, and thirteen years before that in a part-time capacity, the decision to leave has been long in the making. As a member of WUZ, he has been able to use his knowledge of a number of instruments in the interests of a kind of music which particularly appeals to him. While it would be possible to "settle for the easy life," he feels the need of further challenges, the need to play a variety of free-lance dates, and to teach in a less circumscribed atmosphere.

THE "ORPHANS"

The bass-clarinet chair which Viscuglia has left is one of several having unusual status in the orchestra. Listed separately on the players' roster, this instrument joins the piccolo, English horn, contrabassoon, and tuba as being the solo province of one individual. Although E-flat clarinet and timpani are also billed apart from their sections, there is not, somehow, the same aura of isolation that surrounds these five. While the five are close relations to their next-chair neighbors—piccolo to flutes, bass clarinet to clarinets, English horn to oboes, contrabassoon to bassoons, tuba the bottom voice of the trombones—their exclusivity as a group has never been given a collective name within the body of musicians. Surprisingly, they have not been dubbed "les cinq" or "the five horsemen of the Apocalypse," in recognition of their distinct, characteristic missions. "We're orphans," says one such player; "fringe instruments," says another—assessments most listeners are inclined to deny when they hear the unique sounds composers have decided only they should produce.

Lois Schaefer, who plays piccolo in the BSO, might have been a pianist—her mother and grandmother were music teachers—but her early lessons were "a disaster." She might have followed the lead of her sister who was to become a cellist in the BSO and the Philadelphia Orchestra. But when she was growing up in Yakima, Washington, her choice in school was the flute. Coached initially by her school band leader, she later was taught by a flute-oriented violinist. A member of the Yakima Community Orchestra and numerous chamber groups, Lois went to the Interlochen Music Camp. While there, she was offered a scholarship to New England Conservatory for study with Georges Laurent, the BSO's principal flutist.

Before joining the orchestra in 1965, she had extensive experience in the RCA and Columbia Recording Orchestras, with the NBC Opera Company, as principal flute with the New York City Opera, and as assistant principal flute with the Chicago Symphony. A participant in the 1963 Casals Festival, she also joined the Boston Symphony Chamber Players in their tour of the Soviet Union in 1967. Lois has been soloist with the BSO both in Boston and at Tanglewood in Vivaldi concertos for piccolo, and is a member, with Ann Hobson and Carol Procter, of the New England Harp Trio. Her use of a wooden or silver instrument is most often determined by the reaction of the conductor, and as in the case of all wind players, she points out that care of teeth and lips is particularly important. "Look out for dental problems," she warns. Fingers too can present problems—paper cuts and falling icicles can be hazardous, but so far cat scratches have not been a deterrent.

Group lessons in clarinet, offered by the National Institute of

Arts to young aspirants in his native Salt Lake City, started Laurence Thorstenberg on his career as a woodwind player. However, a chance to play oboe in the school band resulted in his turning to that instrument and taking lessons from "one of the best oboists in town." After high school a stint followed in the army, during which he played in bands and orchestras in Europe. Upon release from the army, he first attended Brigham Young University, then the Curtis Institute. A one-year recall to the army during the Korean War was spent on a band tour, after which he resumed his professional career, first as second oboe in the Baltimore Symphony, then as first chair in the Dallas Symphony, and then as assistant first in the Chicago Symphony. In between there was a tour of Russia with the Philadelphia Orchestra, and "the most enjoyable musicmaking ever" in chamber music sessions at Marlboro.

Recommended by Ray Still, first oboe of the Chicago Symphony, Thorstenberg played for Chicago's conductor Fritz Reiner in the ballroom of the Great Northern Hotel in New York in what was practically a "secret audition" since no open notice had been given. "Those were the days when conductors wanted to make their personnel decisions alone," he says, "and pleased as I was to be chosen, I think one of the biggest factors in the improvement of American orchestras is the open audition, judged by players as well."

In Chicago, Thorstenberg took over the English horn in an emergency, and although he owned one, he had never had special training for it. He continued playing it, with increased interest in its differences and in a better pay scale. "Most woodwind players agree the English horn has a greater range of sound than the flute," he declares. "That's influenced by the style of reed-making. I developed my own way, which made a difference in the range of sound types, but while many wind players become neurotic about reed-making, I'm not one of them. Acoustical conditions influence the reed, along with the feeling of the hall or room. Some reeds last for weeks, others for a few days—breaking them in is necessary. I think the more sensitive you are, the more you can make the best of any reed."

Thorstenberg's move from Chicago to Boston was accomplished in an era when musicians were trying to improve their positions on their own against rather formidable odds. When he heard that there would be auditions in Boston for an English horn player to replace the retiring veteran Louis Speyer, he informed the Chicago manager, conductor, and personnel manager that he would be absent on January 19, 1964. On that day in Boston he played in the third preliminary, was selected for the finals, became the number-one choice, and was contracted to join the BSO. However, the then-Chicago management refused to waive a contractual demand of one year's notice for leaving, and Thorstenberg was, upon his return, "suspended from employment." Controversial arbitration was not in his favor, so he was more than eager to join the BSO for its summer at Tanglewood in 1964.

Composers have not been generous with English horn solos—the Sibelius *Swan of Tuonela*, the third movement pastoral duet in Berlioz's *Fantastic Symphony*, and the offstage shepherd's pipe in Wagner's *Tristan and Isolde* are among the notable few. In Colin Davis's recording session of the Sibelius, Thorstenberg recalls going through "The Swan" twice ("without warm-up") after the orchestra had finished taping the first two Sibelius symphonies. "By that time the orchestra pitch had gone up, and I had to meet it," he says. "I didn't hear a playback, but Davis kindly made me a gift of the set which included it. So far I haven't dared to unwrap it." Similarly, Thorstenberg sits onstage through two movements of the Berlioz and then, unsupported, engages in a shepherds' haunting "ranz des vaches" dialogue with an offstage oboe. "I just have to 'psych' myself for going on cold," he declares resignedly.

If Richard Plaster had listened to some early advice ("Don't be a musician if there's anything else you want to do"), he would not have become the BSO's contrabassoon in 1952. Born in a Moravian community in North Carolina, he heard and participated in music from his earliest years. "There's a tradition," Plaster says, "that if you put a horn in a baby's crib and he blows it—let him live." In church services, wind instruments were used instead of organ. Therefore, after study of violin and piano, Richard, like all his contemporaries, began trumpet at the age of nine, and participated in performances of richly traditional religious music. However, a few years later he also learned the bassoon and it was this instrument that caught his lasting affection. From 1942 to 1946, he was a member of the North Carolina Symphony, and from 1946 to 1948 he transferred his performing abilities to the Army Ground Force Band. After study at Davidson College he received B.S. and M.S. degrees from the Juilliard School in 1951. Immediately thereafter, he was engaged by the Baltimore Symphony, where he played for one season before auditioning for the BSO. Charles Munch, bassoonist Allard, concertmaster Burgin, and English horn player Speyer screened the group of finalists from which Plaster was chosen to become contrabassoon in 1952.

Chester Schmitz admits to being "a rare one who took to the tuba and stayed with it." With a mother who played the violin ("too hard for me"), and a father who was a band director, he first studied baritone horn, but gave up music temporarily when he couldn't expend his energy on drums, and settled for football instead. As a high school freshman, Chester took on tuba "because that was all there was left in the band." While still in high school, he performed so well as a substitute in *Petrouchka* that Skrowaczewski, conductor of the Minnesota Orchestra, offered him a contract there. Instead, he continued his musical education at the University of Iowa, and was active in dance, polka, and Dixieland bands before joining the United States Army Band in 1963. However, his army assignment brought him to duty at the White House where as one of the Strolling Strings, which played for state functions, he remained stationary on the sidelines as assistant first bass. A chance substitution in the Richmond Symphony was his only other orchestral experience before he heard of a vacancy in the Boston Symphony in 1965. His audition—the first ever for him—in a field of twenty-five contestants, resulted in his being top choice, so that he joined the BSO in 1966 at the age of twenty-six.

The tuba is involved in two thirds of the orchestral repertory, and with Boston Pops Schmitz has been featured with Julia Child as narrator in George Kleinsinger's novelty piece, *Tubby the Tuba*, telecast from Symphony Hall. Outside, he has performed the Vaughan Williams Tuba Concerto with several orchestras and, like Thorstenberg, senses "a unique responsibility to be able to come in cold on a solo instrument."

As the largest of portable instruments, awkward to handle, the tuba has never "turned him off," since the BSO moves it for all concert engagements, but Schmitz thinks that "one finds a higher degree of talent among musicians whose instruments are easier to carry."

THE PRINCIPALS

Weighty responsibilities, if not weighty instruments, are the lot of the first-desk players—the orchestra's designated principals. As heads of each instrumental section they are primarily responsible for directing the course of strings, winds, brass, and percussion as the conductor conveys his intentions to them. Successors to proven leaders—they are invariably soloists of the first rank as well as skillful technicians, aware of the pitfalls which can occur in the best-rehearsed performance.

Instrumentalists arrive at first-desk positions in unpredictable ways: from within the orchestra itself, where members of the section may compete with outside applicants, or from beyond Symphony Hall, via the auditions route. However, no matter how prominent one's credentials may have been in other symphonic organizations, the winner is selected only on the basis of the audition performance.

Principals occupy more than honorary positions, for it is from them that widely dispersed strings, and interacting choirs of flutes, clarinets, oboes, bassoons, and the percussion battery take instant cues. While everyone necessarily has an eye on the conductor, those musicians placed farthest from the podium necessarily learn to *anticipate* the director's beat in order to "come in" with players seated up front. It is this seemingly minuscule time difference that first-desk leaders must continually take into account to assure perfect coordination from their colleagues.

Leader of the orchestra (he is so designated by title in orchestras abroad) is the concertmaster, the first violinist. Joseph Silverstein, the BSO's occupant of the post since 1961, comments: "There are many roles to play, with heavy responsibilities to one's colleagues and the institution. Sometimes it is difficult to walk that line." As the focal point among the players, he is the official link in rehearsal and performance between the conductor and the body of musicians, as well as principal of the first section of violins. He must be constantly on the alert for untoward occurrences that may beset even the greatest orchestras (and conductors)—many a concertmaster has saved a performance from disaster by quick thinking when an unpredictable chain of mishaps has threatened to disrupt it. There are still veteran players who remember a tour performance long ago when the music director inexplicably became lost in the middle of Wagner's "Forest Murmurs," and it took heroic measures on the part of a former concertmaster, not only to keep the music going, but to have everyone finish together. Fortunately, such occurrences are so unusual as to assume legendary status immediately.

Silverstein's progress to the BSO concertmaster's chair was not an overnight happening. Inheritor of a family tradition of violin-making and performance, he took to the instrument without urging, studying in his native Detroit before going on to Curtis Institute. Three years in the Houston Symphony, one year in the Philadelphia Orchestra, and one year with the Denver Symphony, where he was concertmaster and assistant conductor, preceded his joining the Boston Symphony in 1955—at age twenty-three—as a member of the second violin section. Although at the time it was unprecedented, he was granted leave in 1959 to compete in the Queen Elizabeth International Competition in Belgium, where he was awarded third place. The following year, coincidentally to his being moved to the BSO's first violin section, he won the prestigious Walter W. Naumburg Award in New York, which carried with it a Town Hall recital debut and the promise of solo and orchestral engagements.

It was the suggestion of Charles Munch, then the BSO's music director, that Silverstein leave to pursue a career as a soloist. However, he recalls, "I felt my career was based in this orchestra, so I wrote a letter to Mr. Cabot [Henry B. Cabot, president of the BSO board of trustees], saying I'd like to stay if I could be assured a chance to compete for the post of concertmaster, should the chair become vacant." Apparently impressed by the candor of the letter, Cabot recommended to the music director-designate, Erich Leinsdorf, that he be heard, along with all other BSO players interested in the position, when it became available late in 1961. As a result of open auditions, Silverstein was chosen to succeed Richard Burgin, who was retiring after forty-two years as concertmaster, and he moved to the first chair with the beginning of the Leinsdorf regime in 1962–1963.

Another first-desk player to work her way forward from the last stand is Marylou Speaker, principal of the second section of violins. She recalls that her first BSO audition, for a fellowship in the Berkshire Music Center, took place in her native Oregon, where she was heard by Erich Leinsdorf, then leading the orchestra on a transcontinental tour. Subsequently, she spent student summers at Tanglewood, Aspen, and Marlboro, having enrolled at New England Conservatory. While a student there, she was one of four finalists for a BSO vacancy, but, in her words, "still green behind the ears," she was called upon for something she hadn't prepared, and the position went elsewhere. Thereafter, she embarked on a period of graduate study at the University of California, and freelanced in and around Los Angeles, playing Hollywood studio assignments, chamber music, and solo engagements "to become good enough to be in the BSO." In 1970, the orchestra invited her to audition for an upcoming opening, which she did—successfully—and began her career there in the last chair of the second violins. Retirement of William Marshall as assistant principal of the section in 1974 resulted in her winning this position by audition, and in 1977–1978, she succeeded to the post of principal, also by audition, replacing Victor Yampolsky who left the orchestra to become conductor of the Atlantic Symphony in Halifax, Nova Scotia.

Principal cellist Jules Eskin and first violist Burton Fine are both Philadelphians who received musical training at Curtis Institute—Eskin under Gregor Piatigorsky and Leonard Rose, but Fine as a violinist under Ivan Galamian. Before his Curtis days, Eskin had, at sixteen, been a member of the Symphony in Dallas, where he studied with Janos Starker. After Curtis a three-year army stint preceded his winning the 1954 Naumburg Award, and its complementary recital debut at New York's Town Tall. A participant in both the Casals Festivals in Puerto Rico and the Marlboro Festivals, he was principal cellist with the New York City Opera and New York City Ballet before his three-year engagement as first cellist with the Cleveland Orchestra. He joined the BSO as principal cello in 1964.

Although he never officially studied viola, Fine recalls an informal chamber music program at Curtis where "there would be a viola on the piano for anyone who wanted to try it." Availing himself of this opportunity among a plethora of less adventurous violinists, he became the temporary violist at many of these sessions. As a consequence he "learned the whole viola chamber music literature." A sudden switch to the University of Pennsylvania for an A.B. in chemistry and a Ph.D. from the Illinois Institute of Technology resulted in a nine-year period as a research chemist in the National Aeronautics and Space Administration in Cleveland. Although he continued to play violin and chamber music in his spare time, he made a decision in 1963 to return to music. This determination led to his audition and acceptance as a member of the second violin section of the Boston Symphony. The following year, in widely advertised auditions for the vacant first violist spot, Fine was the winner. Although he had never played the instrument in the orchestra, the viola on the Curtis piano had indeed proved its staying power.

A recent addition to Boston Symphony's first-desk players is Edwin Barker who, at age twenty-four, became principal bass in 1977. In elementary school, verbal confusion between bass drums, which he wanted to learn, and double bass, which seemed appropriate for a tall nine-year-old with large hands, resulted in his being assigned the big stringed instrument instead. His first teacher, a violist, taught him bass according to viola-cello technique, and his progress was so marked that he decided to become a professional musician. Studying at New England Conservatory with former BSO principal Henry Portnoi, he played in the school's symphony, contemporary music and ragtime ensembles, as well as with Boston Pops, the Albany Symphony, and the Lake George Summer Opera. While still a senior, he auditioned first for the New York Philharmonic, then the Chicago Symphony. As cofinalist with another player, he was invited by the New York orchestra to alternate in the open position during the 1975 season, which he did briefly before returning by choice to complete his last year at the Conservatory. Meanwhile, his Chicago audition had won him a post in the bass section, which he joined before graduation in January 1976. Word of Henry Portnoi's retirement as principal first bass of the BSO brought him back to Boston again to compete for his teacher's former position. He was adjudged first-place winner and joined the orchestra as first-desk double bass in 1977.

The appearance of women members on the rosters of major American symphonies was a slow-moving process. In Boston a few played sporadically but none became principals until Doriot Anthony Dwyer was engaged as first flute in 1952. "Women at that time were not encouraged generally," she recalled in a news interview later, "so by and large they weren't as good as men. Nobody expected them to do as well. I thought I'd try out for the Boston Symphony but I never expected to get it." Relative of a pioneer feminist, Susan B. Anthony, and daughter of a flutist who had played professionally and was her first teacher, Mrs. Dwyer came naturally to the instrument. "My mother never pressured me, but she played so well herself that it was a stimulus." Membership in her high school band, and further study with Ernest Liegl, first flute of the Chicago Symphony, preceded her going on to the Eastman School of Music, where she worked with Joseph Mariano.

After graduation from Eastman, she began her professional career in the National Symphony in Washington, toured with the Ballet Russe de Monte Carlo, and joined the Los Angeles Philharmonic as second flute. For his summer engagement as music director of the Hollywood Bowl Orchestra, Bruno Walter chose her to play principal flute. During this time, she sent out many letters signed *Miss* Doriot Anthony, requesting to be informed of orchestra auditions, "but most didn't even write back." However, when she heard that Georges Laurent was retiring after three decades as the BSO's principal flutist, she applied and was invited with others to play for Charles Munch, Laurent, and then-concertmaster Richard Burgin. After a period of concentrated preparation and a certain amount of secrecy, she made the trip east, auditioned at Tanglewood, then returned home to wait.

The engagement call came, and with it a flurry of publicity. "In Los Angeles it became a 'scandal' when their second became the BSO's first," she remembers. In Boston, too, the engagement of a woman principal for the first time by its orchestra made the headlines. However, when one interviewer pointed out that women also occupied first chairs in Houston, St. Louis, and Chicago, Mrs. Dwyer was not taken aback. "If a woman is proficient, I believe she usually gets what she wants," she countered.

Traditionally, though without reasonable explanation, tensions often exist within the close-clustered group of virtuoso woodwind principals. Sometimes the "neurotic" business of reed-making is blamed, along with a subconscious resentment against those who do not have to perform this task. Sometimes the necessity of weaving interlocking solo passages is thought responsible. The engagement of Mrs. Dwyer in the chauvinistic 1950s ("I used to hate you girls," one now-repentant colleague is said to have confessed) might have increased these tensions. However, such turned out not to be the case and the BSO's quartet of first-desk winds has shown remarkable solidarity through the years.

Preceding Mrs. Dwyer's arrival by two years, Ralph Gomberg joined the BSO as principal oboe in 1950 after having played first desk with the Baltimore Symphony, the New York City Center Symphony, and the Mutual Broadcasting Orchestra. Youngest of seven children in a highly musical family, he was one of five to graduate from Curtis Institute, and at fourteen had been the youngest pupil ever of Marcel Tabuteau, noted oboist of the Philadelphia Orchestra. When Leopold Stokowski formed the All American Youth Orchestra in 1940, he chose Ralph, then eighteen, as principal oboe. Nine years later he was accepted by Charles Munch for the post of principal oboe in the BSO; his brother, Harold Gomberg, occupied the same post with the New York Philharmonic for many years until his recent retirement.

Playing the oboe, Ralph says

... is like a strong man trying to juggle eggs without breaking them. At a performance, audience reaction starts "the juices" and in spite of nervousness or first night jitters, you wait for special moments of satisfaction, and you have them. Everyone's shape of lips and concept of sound is different. The reed is the heart and soul of the oboe—without it, it's simply a pipe—and the making of the reed distinguishes the tone of the oboe, like a fingerprint. Besides, the oboe gives the "A" to the orchestra—everyone hates you for that!

First clarinetist Harold ("Buddy") Wright came by the instrument that from the first "fit" him because his mother asked his high school band leader what her two sons should play. (His brother became a trumpeter.) Proximity to Philadelphia permitted him to study there with Ralph McClane, first clarinet of the Philadelphia Orchestra, and he had entered Westchester, Pennsylvania, State Teachers College when the army beckoned. Although his career in the service was brief, he played cymbals and bass drum

When schedules permit, BSO musicians enjoy changing their tune by playing opera. Here, with violinists Marylou Speaker and Leo Panasevich (foreground, center), are colleagues Fredy Ostrovsky, Harvey Seigel, Vyacheslav Uritsky, and Ronald Knudsen.

(Top) *Charles Kavalovski, whose career is divided between being first desk French horn with the BSO and a university professor of physics, allots at least two hours a day to practice.*

(Bottom) *First desk clarinetist Harold Wright joined the BSO in 1970 after playing in several major American orchestras and participating in the Casals and Marlboro Music Festivals.*

Harry Ellis Dickson and first flutist Doriot Anthony Dwyer rehearse a virtuoso number programmed for Youth Concerts at Symphony Hall.

in an army band before being promoted to drum major. After being discharged, he continued his musical studies at the Curtis Institute, and subsequently was engaged by the orchestras of Houston, Dallas, and Washington, D.C. In Washington he was principal clarinet from 1951 to 1970, and it was there that he met his wife Ruth, a flutist. For sixteen summers they have participated in the Marlboro Festival in Vermont, and both there and at the Casals Festivals in Puerto Rico, Buddy worked with the renowned cellist. His last Marlboro appearance took place in 1974 when he was a member of a Mozart quintet that played music in memory of Casals. Wright was chosen principal clarinet of the BSO in 1970. In addition to membership in the Boston Symphony Chamber Players, he teaches at Boston University. His recordings of chamber music are numerous, and he has joined with a group of BSO colleagues to form a woodwind quintet that will make a sponsored tour of Japan in the spring of 1979. Although he admits that his sons had piano "crammed down their throats," the elder, a student at the Massachusetts Institute of Technology, has adopted viola as an avocation, and the younger, a preteenager, is veering toward the clarinet.

Sherman Walt's interest in the bassoon was instilled initially by his high school music instructor in Virginia, Minnesota, and furthered by his mother, a theater pianist in silent film days. His progress on the instrument was so remarkable that it came to the attention of Dmitri Mitropoulos, then music director of the Minneapolis (later Minnesota) Symphony, during an orchestra-sponsored competition for young musicians. The conductor himself underwrote Walt's musical training at the University of Minnesota until he went on to Curtis Institute in Philadelphia, where Ferdinand Del Negro and Marcel Tabuteau were among his teachers. Military service during World War II, for which he was awarded the Bronze Star, was followed on his return to civilian life by his engagement as first bassoon of the Chicago Symphony. He remained at Chicago until 1953 when he became the BSO's principal bassoonist. In addition to membership in the Boston Symphony Chamber Players, he is a professor of music at Boston University and a faculty member of the Berkshire Music Center.

Like first violist Burton Fine, Charles Kavalovski, principal horn of the BSO since the summer of 1972, is a successful scientist who opted for a career in music. In conjunction with musical studies, he obtained a Ph.D. degree in nuclear physics, and has since done scientific research at the University of Minnesota, the University of Washington, and at M.I.T. He played principal horn with the Denver Symphony in 1969 and in 1970–1971. Prior to joining the BSO, he was first horn with the Spokane Symphony in Washington, as well as professor of physics at Washington State College. Since coming to Boston, he has been both adjunct professor in physics and adjunct professor of music at Boston University, but, in his words, "the BSO was a once-in-a-lifetime opportunity, so I operate two careers concurrently. For the past twenty years I've played horn two or three hours daily, which has been possible perhaps because I've never owned a TV set. I must program my time carefully, for while physics remains an intellectual challenge, the horn is closer to the heart."

Another principal from a musical family is Armando Ghitalla. Growing up in Illinois in his musical Italian family was all that was needed to set him on a performing course that began with cornet at age eight and led to his study of trumpet in high school and at Illinois Wesleyan University before joining the navy in World War II. He resumed training for a performing career thereafter, attending New York University and the Juilliard School, where he studied trumpet with William Vacchiano. Professional engagements followed after he received a B.S. degree, as first trumpet with the New York City Opera and Ballet Companies, the RCA

Recording Orchestra, Paul Lavelle's Band of America, and the Houston Symphony. He was engaged by the Boston Symphony in 1951, and became principal trumpet in 1965. He has recorded for Cambridge Records, and appeared as soloist with orchestras in London, Richmond, Virginia, and Portland, Maine.

Although his first inclination had been toward the trumpet, principal trombonist Ronald Barron was influenced by his father to play the trombone in his sixth-grade band in Harrisburg, Pennsylvania. Fortunately, "the band ended up with a trombone player who found that as he got older he enjoyed it more and more. Now it is a great part of me!" He furthered his musical studies with Ernest Glover at the Cincinnati College-Conservatory of Music before playing with the Montreal Symphony. In 1970 he joined the trombone section of the BSO. In 1974 he was winner of the highest prize awarded to trombone at the international competition for instrumentalists in Munich, where he appeared as soloist with the Bavarian Radio Orchestra. The following year he was winner of auditions for the post of principal trombone in the BSO, and has since recorded albums of contemporary French and turn-of-the-century American trombone selections.

Principal timpanist Everett Firth (known to his colleagues only as Vic), was reared in Maine, where his father was a supervisor of music in the schools and also a trumpeter. At four, Vic started trumpet lessons with him, but by age twelve he had switched to percussion, taught by a colleague of his father. In his teens, he came to Boston to study at the drum school run by George Stone, then proceeded to New England Conservatory where Lawrence White and Roman Szulc, his BSO predecessor, were his teachers. He also studied with a future BSO colleague, Charles Smith, with Saul Goodman of the New York Philharmonic, and attended the Berkshire Music Center where he met his future wife, a cellist. Vic was twenty-one when he was hired by Charles Munch to join the

BSO in 1952 as bass drummer. When he was appointed principal timpanist in 1956, he was the youngest musician to gain a first chair since 1898.

However, reflecting on the experience in an interview twenty years later in *Drums Unlimited News,* Firth said: "It takes a mature man to pay attention to nuance, balance, and phrasing, and to create elegant shape." In action with the BSO, he admits striving to do everything with style, "to arrive at the great insight one needs in order to get a definitive performance—that's when the experience gets rewarding."

As senior member now in length of tenure, first harpist Bernard Zighéra has participated in many definitive performances, and has seen a procession of first-desk musicians since joining the orchestra in 1926. When he auditioned for Koussevitzky in Paris, he played both piano and harp, instruments in which he had won top honors at the Conservatoire National several years before. Prior to his audition, he was a member of the Société des Concerts and the Paris Opera orchestra. When he received the music director's invitation to join the BSO shortly thereafter, he found himself engaged not only as principal harp but as pianist for the orchestra—posts he occupied dually for eighteen years.

Although preceded to Boston in 1925 by his cellist brother Alfred Zighéra, who had joined the BSO under Pierre Monteux, Bernard went his separate way. Mentioning to Koussevitzky that he had nowhere to practice the lengthy piano parts assigned him in Stravinsky's *Petrouchka* and Loeffler's *Pagan Poem,* he was surprised when almost immediately a concert grand appeared at the door of his modest Boston apartment. Because of the piano's size, it had to be hoisted up and through his window, thereby gaining for him instant neighborhood celebrity.

A recipient of membership in the French Legion of Honor, Zighéra, in addition to his duties with the BSO, organized and conducted a series of chamber music concerts in Boston between 1936 and 1941. According to report, when Harpo Marx sought to become his pupil, he declared he had "nothing to teach him." He has, however, been a faculty member at New England Conservatory since 1927, as well as a founding member of the Berkshire Music Center since its inception.

And so as its history lengthens, the Boston Symphony plays host to an ever-variegated cast of "chosen ones," who make their entrances (and their exits) and play many parts. Most of them come with the hope of staying, since to be there represents the supreme effort of a lifetime. After arrival, they soon find themselves among friends of mutual choosing—it's difficult to be a loner within a group of one hundred or so engaged constantly in a common effort—and although each maintains individuality as a professional worker, the structure of the orchestra bespeaks a camaraderie not to be found elsewhere. Some of them may fight it, others may sink contentedly into the security it offers, but the majority retain the concert-by-concert excitement that this community of sound can provide.

III

The Orchestra in Action

LIFE AT SYMPHONY HALL

During the regular BSO season in Symphony Hall, the public may hear the orchestra as many as four times a week, plus an open rehearsal. Not all of the twenty-two weeks have the same number of concerts scheduled—the eight open rehearsals are distributed throughout the season, there are occasional runouts (performances played outside Symphony Hall on a one-day round-trip basis). However, between late September and the end of April, the musicians play more than one hundred concerts and public rehearsals in Boston alone. Actual performance time averages between six and seven hours each week, but this hardly represents the whole story.

Listeners who come to Symphony after a nine-to-five working day often have the impression that the body of instrumentalists, because of their expertise, gather together and play extemporaneously for the public's pleasure. Nothing could be further from the fact. The life of the BSO member is as stringent as that of any hard worker. It is a six-days-out-of-seven job, with strictly determined hours of rehearsal preparation. The works of Beethoven, for instance—his name alone is graven on Symphony Hall's proscenium—might seem to be graven similarly on the minds of any experienced orchestral performer. But every different conductor or soloist brings distinctive interpretation to a performance, and it is the business of each player to lend his or her particular skill to the changing concept. This, of course, is welded into musical shape long before audiences settle into place for a Friday afternoon, Thursday morning, or weekday evening concert.

As the Boston Symphony moves toward its second century, the rehearsal and concert procedures which have been formulated to assure its greatness are the result of a combined effort on the part of players and management to see eye-to-eye in the interests of superlative performance. In the beginning it was not so. Wilhelm Gericke, musical director of the BSO (1884–1889), quoted in M. A. DeWolfe Howe's *The Boston Symphony Orchestra, 1881–1931*, recalled rather plaintively:

Before I came to Boston, members of the Orchestra had been used to a great deal of freedom; for instance, members living out of town were allowed to leave the rehearsal at twelve in order to be home for lunch; or to reach a train for another out-of-town engagement of their own—whether the rehearsal was finished or not. It was not easy to make them understand that their engagement for the Boston Symphony Concerts had to be considered first and foremost, and that the rehearsal had to be finished before everything else.[1]

While the situation improved for Gericke and his successors, rehearsals proved to be a continuing sticking point well into the present century. A succession of music directors used whatever time they felt necessary, but it was not until the arrival of Serge Koussevitzky in 1924 that the issue got under the skin of the players. Eventually the maestro instituted a custom of Thursday morning rehearsals to which members of the press and special guests were invited. In the recollection of a retired BSO musician, "Koussey was impossible. He would rail against individual players and put on a fiery temperamental show," leaving the orchestra shaken and exhausted. "Then afterward he would tell us how much he loved us!" Such excesses, of course, led to reforms specifying the extent of rehearsal time. However, those who were involved still recall a certain "fear of God" when reminding Koussevitzky that the allotted period had ended.

Today, in the meticulously negotiated Trade Agreement between players and management, BSO rehearsal and performance commitments are spelled out and adhered to without disagreement or rancor. Each player has a contract with the Boston Symphony Orchestra Corporation. In each contract the maximum number of "quota services" (i.e., rehearsals and concerts) is indicated. The BSO year specifically consists of a Symphony season, followed by a Pops Concert series, and a summer season at Tanglewood. First-desk players are not involved in the Pops season but, as members of the Boston Symphony Chamber Players, tour during the period that follows the Symphony season. Each BSO musician receives one week of paid vacation during both Symphony and Pops seasons. Four weeks of paid vacation are given between the summer and Symphony seasons, with an additional "floating week" to be scheduled by the BSO Corporation during the year. A system of free days, along with payment for overtime and extra services, is also specified in the Agreement. An "optional" release period (if one wishes to leave the Symphony) is further subject to negotiation between artist and management.

Backstage, one week in advance, symphony musicians will find a posted schedule of rehearsal times and numbers to be played. This is a confirmation of an earlier informational schedule, subject to change, made available by the management two weeks ahead. Rehearsal time is set at two and a half hours, with a twenty-minute intermission some time after the first hour or hour and a half. Orchestra rehearsals at Symphony Hall usually begin at 10:00 A.M., but musicians habitually arrive some time before that to "warm up."

Harry Ellis Dickson, violinist in the BSO since 1938, assistant conductor of Boston Pops, music director of Youth Concerts at Symphony Hall, author of *"Gentlemen, More Dolce Please!,"* and raconteur extraordinaire, tells what one might hear in the offstage Tuning Room:

There is a traditional bedlam of sound in the Tuning Room before an orchestra concert, beginning quietly some time before the concert when the ambitious ones arrive, and reaching an almost unbearable crescendo just before concert time, for no musician will ever go onstage without warming up.

The "frustrated Heifetz" comes early, sets himself firmly in the middle of the Tuning Room and by the time his colleagues have arrived to drown him out he has already played two recitals. The horn players (and this is a comparatively new technique) blast away as loud as they can, while the oboists give them dirty looks as they try to blow a few discreet notes, remove the reed, curse it, shave it, put it back, and blow a few more unsatisfactory notes. There seems to be a contest continually between the oboists and the clarinetists as to who will change reeds more often, for no one amongst them has ever found a perfect one.

Richard Burgin, our former marvelous concertmaster, was never heard to practice any fast passages in the Tuning Room. As a matter of fact, unlike the Tuning Room Virtuoso Syndrome of today, Burgin seemed almost amateurish as he practiced "sliding" from one note to another.

Drummers, fortunately, do not practice backstage on their instruments. They walk around with their sticks in their hands looking for an empty chair to practice on, or a blank wall, or a phone book.

If all this seems slightly ludicrous, it is not. Musicians are the most serious, conscientious people in the world. Their lives are dedicated to their instruments and to making those instruments do their bidding in their attempts to bring some beauty into this troubled world.

An "onstage" call to the rehearsal, as to a performance, is given five minutes before starting time, followed by the traditional tuning procedure. The players' Trade Agreement specifies fines to be paid to the Pension Institution for unexcused absences or tardiness not proven to be beyond the absentee's control.

Musicians' chairs have been arranged onstage by stage manager Al Robison and his crew according to the requirements of the first piece to be rehearsed. Placement of chairs for the cello section requires special care. Each cellist has his or her own chair—the seat a designated height from the floor, and often furnished with a cushion of just the right thickness. Individual folders containing the parts of the day's program have been provided for each stand (strings share a stand, or desk, in pairs; winds, brass, harp, and percussion use single stands), having been appropriately sorted out and allotted by librarian Victor Alpert, through whose hands pass something approaching 365,000 sheets of music annually.

Being principal librarian of the Boston Symphony involves more than passing out the daily bill of fare to hungry musicians and conductors. To obtain and prepare orchestral parts and scores (many of rare or transient nature must be rented), to add to the orchestra's large permanent collection when the opportunity offers, to arrange exchanges of music with other orchestras, and to undo the inevitable wear-and-tear that markings, greasy fingers, and torn pages can wreak on much-used instrumental parts accounts for only some of the long hours spent in Symphony Hall's overflowing library and labyrinthine storage room. Guest conductors often come with their own material, while the special needs of some—Erich Leinsdorf's fifty-two minutes of *Parsifal*, and Boris Goldovsky's decision to do Mozart's fragmentary *Zaide* at Tanglewood—have called upon Alpert's detective and reconstruction abilities. "If I don't know, I make it up," he says philosophically. "Everything has happened at least once before." His anticipation of the unlikely has paid off more than once.

A native Bostonian, New England Conservatory graduate, and violist in the Indianapolis and Minneapolis symphonies before joining the BSO in 1953, Victor had also toured as principal viola and personnel manager with Arthur Fiedler. With his violinist wife he crossed the continent in an early tour of *Porgy and Bess.* Hired into the library as a musical expert, he was briefly assistant before succeeding to the post of principal librarian. Now, two musically knowledgeable librarians—William Shisler and James Harper—assist Alpert in filling the increasingly varied demands made on this department.

Music for upcoming programs is available to the players a week in advance, so if problems are presented by certain compositions, members of the orchestra may borrow them from the library to take home for practice purposes. Invariably, someone will forget to bring back his or her part for the first rehearsal or even for a performance, but Alpert, himself an experienced musician, has learned to be prepared for such exigencies. Miraculously, a duplicate is produced along with a gently admonishing glance, so the missing part is remembered next time.

Rehearsals, except for the eight open ones at Symphony Hall and those on Saturday mornings at Tanglewood (proceeds from all of which benefit the Pension Fund), are otherwise private affairs between orchestra and conductor. The formality of the concert is absent, dress is casual, and emphasis is placed on accomplishing as much as possible in the time allotted. For the guest conductor, it is the one opportunity to convey programmatic ideas, preferably through actions rather than words. For the musicians, it is an indication of the kind of performance that will emerge as a result of the ambience induced by a stranger on the podium. "We didn't need to be told to try harder," a violinist remarked of a one-time visitor, "when it was obvious from the first that it was *he* who should try harder."

And there are the wiser ones, like the maestro who began the rehearsal for his second week of guesting by addressing the orchestra: "I so enjoyed the concert last night. If you have to make music, that's the way to do it." Needless to say, he received the tribute of unanimous shuffling of feet—the musicians' traditional approving applause for something they like to hear.

On a person-to-person basis with a familiar guest conductor, unvarnished frankness is sometimes traded between players and conductor. "Do you really mean what you say?" a section man asks. "I bloody well do," is the reply from the podium, and the rehearsal proceeds without undue rancor.

For the standard repertory, whether with the music director or a guest conductor, rehearsals provide players a chance to absorb the individualistic nuances that distinguish one interpretation from another. Questions and answers are exchanged, notes are corrected, and reminders are marked on the parts, so that the musician is prepared for his or her own role in the performance.

Formation in 1970 of the Tanglewood Festival Chorus, under John Oliver's direction, provides the orchestra with a year-round body of 120 voices for choral works. For large-scale works the New England Conservatory choruses, Harvard-Radcliffe choral organizations, and the Boston Boy Choir may participate as well. Rehearsal with the chorus demands an intense concentration, since not only are vocalists involved, but usually solo instruments and sectional passages are interwoven throughout the musical fabric of the piece, with a resultant need for meticulous balance. For each musician as for each singer in the chorus, there is an individual obligation to grasp the conductor's overall concept so the work becomes a coordinated whole.

A BSO rehearsal, then, is a business proposition from which the mask of glamour is dropped. Depending upon who is on the podium, it can be a time of stimulating accomplishment, or a period of endless boredom. Minutes spent by the conductor verbally thrashing out a particular passage with a few players often give way to restiveness among those not involved. Conversations begin, and often when the conductor is ready to proceed, he finds it difficult to silence them. "You are taking my time with your talking," one guest maestro admonished. "*Our* talking?" was an anonymous comment deep within the orchestra.

One player who has rehearsed under three BSO music directors finds that at least two of them were tolerant of musicians' fripperies—sotto voce jokes, artistic doodling on the margins of instrumental parts, long-distance sign-language conversations, staring at the ceiling, and so on. One of these maestros, however, seemed to direct his rehearsal tirades exclusively at unsuspecting guest vocalists, for whom their instrumental colleagues could only shudder collectively and in silence.

Koussevitzky, renowned for his temperamentally low boiling point, would summarily bring rehearsals to an end when a musician or a persistently troublesome passage aroused his ire. Charles Munch, his successor, was his complete antithesis. To quote violinist Harry Ellis Dickson: "... he hated to rehearse, thereby endearing himself to musicians. After rehearsing a few bars of a piece he would invariably stop and say 'Pas necessaire,' and go on to something else."

One recent guest conductor from abroad, a first-time and apparently appreciative visitor, departed from customary procedure during an early rehearsal when he left stage-center and wandered at random through sections of the orchestra, savoring the instrumental sound. Such unusual behavior, of course, was food for the numerous symphonic wits. "This is the kind of conductor I like," said one, "all you have to follow is his shoes," while another warned, "He'd better not do that too often—he might be mugged!" The friendly maestro, however, also possessor of an unconventional free-form beat, became a favorite with the members, who played for him with wholehearted gusto.

Many rehearsal stories have been recorded, amusing, stultifying, or shocking, as the case may be. But there are times when the progress-toward-perfection process evokes a response less easily defined. The late G. Wallace Woodworth, a legendary observer of and participant in musical Boston, recalled in his book, *The World of Music*, a Koussevitzky-BSO rehearsal of Vincent D'Indy's *Istar Variations*, which concluded with a "glowing" *tutti* passage—"a balanced, steady *mezzo forte* with no rise or fall, moving serenely through the epilogue to a luminous F-major ending." Koussey belabored the orchestra, section by section, to achieve the ultimate effect. "Finally he put down his stick and said, 'Gentlemen, you give me a sonority of clarinets, and a sonority of bassoons, a sonority of violas, a sonority of trumpets.' And then with a great encircling gesture, 'It must be *a sonority of gold*.' The most precise technical directions, addressed to a most expert body of professional musicians, had not done the trick; but ... the extraordinary sound ... was somehow achieved by Koussevitzky's flash of imaginative description."

Rehearsals must end, and the performances be given for which they are the preparation. Now the public face of the orchestra is revealed, as a whole new image is acted out upon the stage.

There is a dress code musicians are asked to follow, which differs for afternoon and evening Symphony concerts, the Pops, and Tanglewood performances. The specifying of a "uniform" is not an attempt at regimentation, as some might think, but the result of long-time observation that listener concentration is greater when there are no unusual sartorial details to distract the audience eye.

For afternoon and evening Symphony concerts, women are asked to wear a long black gown with long sleeves. For matinees, men wear black business suits, white shirts, and gray four-in-hand ties; in the evening, black tails, white shirts, black cummerbunds, white tie, and as in the afternoons, black socks and shoes.

A present longtime member of the BSO remembers sporting a pair of shiny black leather loafers on the Symphony Hall stage when this was a novel style in footwear, only to meet the reproving glance of the orchestra manager and be told to go and never sin again. Oboist Wayne Rapier recalls a story about a player and the music director of another orchestra: In the course of a lengthy symphony, a first-desk musician became conscious of the maestro's dark frowns in his direction, accompanied by frantic lunges with his baton. The puzzled player dug in even harder but despite his best musical efforts the conductor's obvious displeasure continued. Finally, at his wits' end, he raised a despairing, questioning face, whereupon, with one more low thrust of the baton, the maestro hissed, "BLUE *ss-socks-ss!*"

Thus, serious consideration is given to visual as well as aural impressions made on the platform. The lady performer who was asked by the management to substitute something more conventional for the snug black pantsuit she had chosen to wear onstage during the orchestra's Far East tour may have had her vanity injured, but she learned that Japanese acceptance of visiting musicians' abilities also includes adherence to their own traditional standards of dress.

The ritual of the orchestral concert seemingly has not changed too much over the years, from the traditional sounding of the "A" by the oboe for tuning, to the concertmaster's signal to musicians to disperse after final acknowledgment of the listeners' applause. Only programs and the response of the audience to them are different every time.

Former music director Charles Munch wrote in *I Am a Conductor:*

The public comes to concerts to hear good performances of beautiful music just as it goes to museums to look at beautiful pictures or statues. It comes to be enriched, instructed, fortified. It does not come to criticize. It comes to take its place in the trinity with the composer and the performer. I am speaking of course of a "good" public, which listens thoughtfully and receptively to good music and good interpreters.... If you make your programs too long, you will weary your audience. Music requires a state of high nervous tension on the part of both listener and performer. Don't overstrain it. A concert should not ordinarily have much more than seventy-five minutes of music if you do not want to hear the rustling of inattention or the noise of seats slamming behind you.

For the experienced professional musician, the innate excitement of performance is ever present. Much of the responsibility for maintaining this excitement, according to concertmaster Silverstein, lies with the interaction of first-desk principals: A certain characteristic of all orchestras is the degree of being one body.

Style may be influenced by individual players within the orchestra—the consistency and beauty of Buddy Wright's phrasing, for instance, has its effect on all sections. In the absence of a conductor capable of making a strong musical statement, these artists can assert themselves and come to the rescue by reacting to one another with the best they have to give. In such circumstances, I think the BSO is, overall, the strongest orchestra in every respect. Most guest conductors don't try to bring about changes in style, therefore the orchestra relies on woodwinds—they're fed by the artistry of these sections.

Principals of the string sections—violins, violas, and basses—with almost half the total population of the orchestra to lead—must work together in behalf of a very audible majority, widely dispersed on the concert platform.

Burton Fine describes his function as head of the viola section:

The principal keeps bowings in order within the section, in accord with the other strings, except when there is good reason not to. Being close to the conductor, we sense the subtleties of his intentions, and represent him to the people behind, who follow. It's necessary to be flexible in a lot of ways, to be receptive to others' suggestions for bowing, and otherwise make life easy for maintaining harmony within the section. When a conductor proves to be hard to follow, we zero in on the concertmaster.

With winds, brass, and percussion, the interplay within smaller sections is more cogently resolved in performance. Players are side by side in their own intimate enclaves, so that distance from their colleagues' sound doesn't present the problems encountered by last-stand strings, or the fringe forest of double basses.

How all these musicians respond depends, of course, on the reaction of each to the maestro before them, and it is possible that the adage is only slightly exaggerated which claims every orchestra to be composed of one hundred conductors.

When the orchestra performs, of course, audience, critics, and even performers have their own responses to the music. From its earliest years the Boston Symphony introduced unfamiliar music at its own risk, no doubt to the unrecorded grumblings of many. Wilhelm Gericke, who was on the podium, reported:

The public of Boston... will be surprised to hear that in those days... during the first performance of Brahms' Symphony No. 3, the audience left the hall in hundreds, and still more at the first performance of Bruckner's Symphony No. 7 (1887). The same thing happened at the first performance of Strauss's symphony *In Italy* (1888).

As late as the turn of the century, prior to the opening of Symphony Hall, a columnist jokingly suggested that the new building's exits would display signs reading "This Way Out In Case of Brahms."

Even noncontroversial Max Fiedler, the BSO's music director from 1908 to 1912, had his problems when he programmed Scriabin's *Poem of Ecstasy* in 1910. The redoubtable critic H.T.P. wrote in the Boston *Transcript:* "The ultra-moderns all resemble each other. When one of these extreme gentlemen comes at you with a *Poem of Ecstasy* you may be sure of one thing, he is going to use every known instrument, and he is either to whisper vagueness to you à la Debussy, or roar it at you à la Strauss." [2]

During his second term as music director of the BSO (1912–1918), Dr. Karl Muck introduced for the first time three European composers—Ravel (*Mother Goose*) in 1913, and a year later, Stravinsky (*Fireworks*) and Schoenberg (*Five Pieces for Orchestra*). All of them at the time presented ensemble difficulties in preparation, since each had a sternly individualistic idiom, and although Muck expended his customary meticulous care on rehearsals, it was thought that he did so more out of duty and concession to "the critical fraternity" than to personal conviction.

In H. Earle Johnson's *Symphony Hall, Boston*, Olin Downes, then music critic of the Boston *Post*, is quoted after the premiere of Schoenberg's *Five Pieces:*

Dr. Muck's gestures had spoken for themselves. He had rapped peremptorily on the conductor's desk as he opened the score. He had raised his baton, as each piece came to an end without resting on any chord familiar to anyone in the audience, and proceeded without a pause and rather grimly to the next "piece," and at last he bowed several times to the orchestra, as to courageous, skillful colleagues, who had performed a difficult and dangerous task, and ignoring a few well-meant handclaps from the audience, marched off the stage, apparently in an unamiable frame of mind.

Philip Hale, in the Boston *Herald*, reported thus on this early musicianly effort in behalf of audience tolerance: "Nothing was thrown at Dr. Muck and the orchestra. There was no perturbation of Nature to show that Schoenberg's pieces were playing; the sun did not hasten its descent; there was no earthquake shock. It was as it should have been in Boston." [3]

While the orchestra and the public later survived performances of such difficult-to-approach novelties as Copland's *Piano Con-*

certo and Stravinsky's *Rite of Spring*, there was as recently as 1972 a minor in-house revolt occasioned by Charles Wuorinen's Violin Concerto, premiered by the BSO at Tanglewood as part of the summer "festival within a festival" of contemporary music. What Wuorinen had composed was an uninterrupted three-movement work with a continuous polyphonic fabric to be shared on equal dynamic levels by the orchestra and the violin soloist (Paul Zukofsky), whose instrument had a regular violin bridge with a transducer built into it. This was connected to a preamplifier which in turn carried the sound by electronic means to loudspeakers, fortunately without pickup of extraneous noise from the fingerboard.

Thus, probably for the first time in musical history, a concerto soloist had an equal voice in terms of volume with the players who partnered him. What had caused some of the dissension undoubtedly was the mistaken impression that an electric violin—a fake instrument—was being used, as opposed to a device which served to convey the natural violin sound with an intensity matched to that of a full body of musicians. For all but the most conservative listeners, it succeeded technically in this aim, but onstage there remained many doubters, and perhaps also a sense of wounded pride in being outdistanced by artificial means. However, Paul Fromm, champion of contemporary composition, defended the performance of such new music with a quote from Serge Koussevitzky who, when he was reproved for his interest in untried scores, paraphrased Stendhal, saying, "If you do not play the new, eventually you will not have the old." [4]

From October 1971 to April 1974, a new series called Spectrum, the brain child of its then associate conductor, Michael Tilson Thomas, made a valiant attempt to take the figurative starch out of the ritual of concertgoing. Players appeared in colorful shirts and dark skirts or trousers. Thomas prefaced each of the unaccustomed selections, from Gabrieli to Steve Reich, with a few lucid and unpatronizing remarks, while audiences, predominantly youthful, poised themselves for a variety of musical surprises.

As a musical celebration of the United States Bicentennial in 1976, the National Endowment for the Arts, a federal agency, gave grants to six major American orchestras (Boston, Chicago, Cleveland, Los Angeles, New York, and Philadelphia) for commissions to six American composers, their works to be played in a round-robin arrangement by the other five after a premiere by the originally designated commissioner.

John Cage's *Renga with Apartment House 1776* was presented for the first time on September 30, 1976, by the Boston Symphony to inaugurate this series, arousing a predictable flurry of controversy among listeners and performers alike. The two halves of the title indicate two different pieces performed simultaneously by separate groups of instrumentalists and soloists. *Renga* (named for a Japanese poetic form) was presided over by one conductor (Joseph Silverstein) and played by a section of the orchestra at its individuals' improvisational will using the verticals and horizontals of Thoreau drawings as guidelines for pitch and rhythm. *Apartment House*, a more formalized collection of snippets from musical Americana, employed four vocalists and numerous instrumental soloists under Seiji Ozawa's direction. At first hearing, critic Richard Dyer wrote in the Boston *Globe:* "It's significant that I haven't really been able to think of any way to describe the sound of it. The overlapping textures were fascinating to hear, but the continuing coherences of the whole were as elusive as they were probably meant to be."

Earlier, George Crumb's *Echoes of Time and the River (Echoes II), Four Processionals for Orchestra*, was performed by the orchestra both in Boston and at Tanglewood. As in other of Crumb's works, the demands of the score go beyond playing. Orchestra members march across the stage, murmur and whisper specified lines in transit, or in the case of brasses, blow tonelessly through their instruments. As described by a program annotator, "standing to play, the mandolinist exits while echoing the motto of the state of West Virginia." Shrieking strings, croaking nonsense syllables, shouts, and whistles are also indicated as musicians' duties in this piece.

Players' reactions to contemporary demands on their abilities cover a wide spectrum. One experienced musician remarked:

There's no objection to patterns—a flute is a flute, for instance—but instructions to "grunt into the instrument" are sadistic. Partnership between composer and instrumentalist has produced some great music. When a composer makes an instrument his slave, to do what he thinks is important and tone isn't considered, the result is illegitimate. The performer is forced to debase his art. It becomes a case of the portraitist made to paint the kitchen.

Younger members, more accustomed to the vagaries of contemporary composition, accept unconventional assignments with equanimity. "Of course we do what's asked. Why not?" one says. "But whether we're proud of it or not depends on the final impact of the performance. No one likes to feel he's been had by any composer."

While all new works present challenges to the players, some turn out to be more invigorating than others. One such was David Del Tredici's *Final Alice*, a Bicentennial commission first presented by the Chicago Symphony on October 7, 1976, and premiered by the Boston Symphony on April 13, 1978. Part of an ongoing series of works inspired by Lewis Carroll's *Alice in Wonderland* and its sources, *Final Alice*, through the magnitude of its orchestral concept and the use of a single amplified voice (soprano Barbara Hendricks), suddenly plunged the players into a large-scale quasi-operatic ambience, without requiring "demeaning" side activities.

76 COMMUNITY OF SOUND

Since the subject matter concerned the trial of the Knave of Hearts (who allegedly "stole those tarts/And took them quite away!"), interspersed with melodic settings of Carroll verses slyly orchestrated to fit the concept of fantasy, *Alice* offered almost an hour of intricate problems to be solved by conductor Seiji Ozawa and the executants.

The instruments required for *Alice* as listed in the BSO program book indicate the sound spectrum:

The score calls for a soprano-narrator, amplified with a bullhorn or electronic equivalent; a folk-group, also amplified, of two soprano saxophones, mandolin, tenor banjo, and accordion; a whisper-chorus of orchestra members; two piccolos (doubling flute), two flutes (one doubling piccolo), three oboes, English horn (doubling oboe), E-flat clarinet (doubling B-flat clarinet), two B-flat clarinets, bass clarinet (doubling B-flat clarinet), three bassoons, contrabassoon (doubling bassoon), four trumpets, six horns, four trombones, tuba; percussion for eight players and including timpani, triangle, small and large suspended cymbals, hi-hat cymbal, crush cymbals, large tamtam, tambourin, snare drum, tenor drums with and without snares, bass drum, tom-toms, whip, ratchet, temple blocks, large cowbell, anvil, siren, theremin, suspended crotal, glockenspiel, xylophone, marimba, vibraphone, tubular bells, wood and glass wind chimes (several sets of each); celesta, two harps, and strings.

Even though all of these instruments never sounded at the same time, the coordinated effort necessary to keep the dynamic level manageable and in balance with an amplified voice tested the ingenuity of Ozawa, Miss Hendricks, and every member of the augmented orchestra. That it worked for the majority of the audiences (always excepting the inevitable traditionalists) exemplified the high degree of skill and professionalism of each individual participant.

Doubling, which involves playing an instrument other than that usually associated with the performer (and sometimes in addition to it), results in an added stipend for the musician affected—as

(Top) *Some prefer to warm up in solitude. Ralph Pottle finds a deserted passageway in Symphony Hall's basement the ideal spot.*

(Bottom) *Contributing to Tuning Room "bedlam" are, from left, first bassoon Sherman Walt, oboist Alfred Genovese, trombone Norman Bolter, bassoon Roland Small, and tuba Chester Schmitz.*

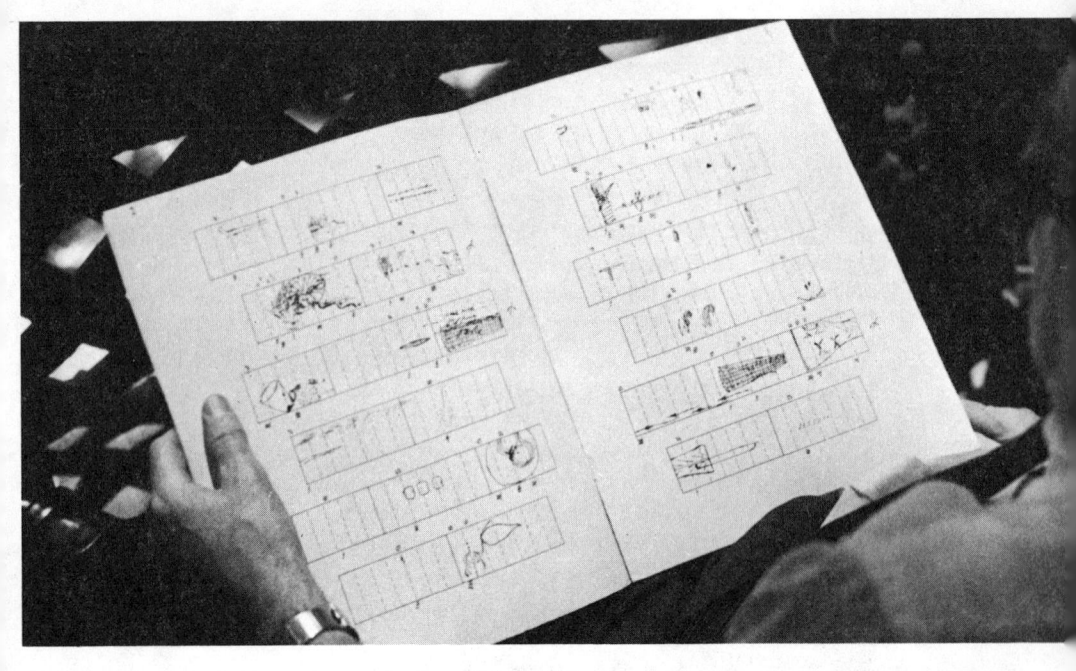

From RENGA by John Cage. Copyright © 1977 by Henmar Press Inc. Reprint permission granted by the publisher.

New scores call for new methods. BSO music director Seiji Ozawa devised unique conducting signals to relay cues for the playing of John Cage's 1976 premiere.

Composer David Del Tredici, associate conductor Joseph Silverstein, and music director Seiji Ozawa discuss the achievement of instrumental balance in preparation for performances of Final Alice *by the BSO.*

piccolo doubling flute, English horn doubling oboe, and so on. However, except as specified in such a score as *Final Alice*, the practice of doubling varies with the artistic taste of the conductor. Where it used to be the custom to double (in this case, multiply by two) certain winds and brass in the Beethoven symphonies for greater balance with full sections of strings, the feeling of many maestros these days is that a texture more in keeping with the composer's basic intention is obtained by following the original scoring, with a corresponding reduction in the number of strings. However, when William Steinberg conducted Mahler's version of Beethoven's Ninth Symphony with the BSO at Tanglewood in 1973, doubling was again the order of the day, to spectacular effect.

Of the numerous BSO members who play other instruments, probably the champion is assistant first and Pops principal cellist Martin Hoherman. He can, when called upon, perform on celesta, piano, banjo, guitar, saxophone, clarinet, accordion, mandolin, and double bass. Violinist Jerome Rosen is adept on a variety of keyboard instruments, as is violist Betty Benthin, and it was Rosen who induced the eerie theremin sounds in *Final Alice*. Assistant principal bass, Will Rhein, is also principal bass of Boston Pops where his performing skills on a number of electronic jazz instruments are frequently featured. Gordon Hallberg, in the course of his career from school, college, and U.S. Marine bands to orchestras from Florida to Halifax, Nova Scotia, had been called upon to play the full range of brass instruments before joining the Boston Symphony as a trombonist.

Ancient instruments related to those they play in the orchestra are added preoccupations of some: violists Burton Fine and Joseph Pietropaolo continue their interest in the viola d'amore; cellist Carol Procter's study of the viola da gamba has led to solos in BSO performances of Bach's *Saint Matthew Passion* and the Monteverdi *Vespers*; while Laurence Thorstenberg has much use for his mastery of the oboe d'amore in Bach's extensive writing for this instrument.

Percussionists, of course, have expertise in a wide variety of traditional and exotic instruments. These recently have been augmented by contemporary composers with such sound producers as brake drums, tire irons, fire sirens, pistol shots, and bird and animal sounds not scored instrumentally. Percussionist Frank Epstein tells of being commissioned to produce at short notice ten pistols required for a performance of Mamangakis' *Anarchia*, presented by the BSO in 1976 for the International Society for Contemporary Music. Armories, gunsmiths, sporting goods stores, and arms manufacturers were canvassed for the kind of soft bullet needed to make the proper impact—all without result. However, by concert time, Epstein had found what proved to serve admirably —ten starter pistols from a joke store.

Probably the loudest sound of all took place in 1972 when a sixty-inch gong imported from New York was struck in Olivier Messiaen's visionary *Et Exspecto Resurrectionem Mortuorum*. Although its earthshaking reverberations shivered timbers (and unwary subscribers) in Symphony Hall, decibels were dispersed more equitably through Tanglewood's open-sided Shed and thence throughout the Berkshire atmosphere, thereby fulfilling Messiaen's original intent when he composed the piece for "vast spaces: churches, cathedrals, and even for performances in the open air and on mountain heights." [5]

EVENING AT POPS

With the end of the Symphony season, and without the orchestra's first-desk players, eight weeks of Pops rehearsals and concerts begin. For some of those who remain, it is "a welcome, carefree period"—for others, "a horrible way of life." Certainly, in the transformed appearance of Symphony Hall—floor seats replaced by tables and chairs, the walls a lively spring color, the stage hung with shiny bangles and baubles—the formality of the BSO's winter surroundings has vanished. The musicians, in light blue jackets and blouses, are spruced up visually, and if they find some of the music on a typical Pops program less than challenging, the predictably enthusiastic response of the audience is undeniable proof of the pleasure they give.

The post-season of lighter music began in 1885 as "Music Hall Promenade Concerts" in the BSO's first home. According to historian H. Earle Johnson, "Mugs of beer were served, and a rail around the hall divided those come to stay for the music from those who just stopped in for a drink. (Some of these latter were in the way of being questionable characters.)" With the move to Symphony Hall in 1900, the atmosphere became "more refined." He noted that "on May and June evenings when the temperature is up, the age percentage is down, and youth attends in happy pairs."

When Arthur Fiedler became its conductor in 1930, Boston Pops, which had continued pleasantly for forty-five years under seventeen leaders, began a new era of popularity. Born in Boston, the son of violinist Emanuel Fiedler, Arthur was named for Arthur Nikisch, the BSO's third music director. Growing up as a typical American boy, he was more interested in the popular songs of the day than in taking the violin lessons which were inevitable in a family with two violinist uncles also in the BSO. When his father retired from the orchestra, the family returned to Berlin, where Arthur won a scholarship to the Royal Academy of Music, adding piano and conducting to his curriculum.

At age twenty, with World War I looming in Europe, the young Fiedler returned to Boston. He became a member of the BSO under Karl Muck, and remained there first as violinist, then as violist, under Henri Rabaud, Pierre Monteux, and Serge Koussevitzky. His desire to conduct, however, persisted. As a result, he formed the Boston Sinfonietta in 1924 with BSO members and they gave chamber concerts both in Boston and on tour. In 1929, through his own fundraising efforts, he inaugurated the free summer Esplanade Concerts. Leading the Pops was the next logical step.

Fiedler's predecessor at the Pops, according to Johnson, had been "a musician of ultraserious purposes" whose tastes "inclined to the archaic or the cerebral." In retrospect, Alfredo Casella (1927–1929) seems to have been a strange choice, even though "the public still came." Johnson recounts that "at length the Pops audience felt deprived of its traditional fare, and welcomed Mr. Fiedler's broader concept of summer entertainment," which as it evolved "is good for either the Brotherhood of Plasterers or the New England Conservatory Alumni; it consists of a group of light overtures, a concerto, usually for piano, and a sheaf of 'hit' tunes from the reigning musical comedies." While time, taste, and television have since altered this format somewhat, the original concept remains to the continuing delight of audiences in Symphony Hall as well as those outside. Through solid musicianship, a shrewd programming sense, and inherent though unobtrusive showmanship, Fiedler built Boston Pops into a unique institution, unequaled anywhere. Tours, recordings, radio broadcasts, and telecasts have made Fiedler and the Pops household names internationally.

In recent years, there have been additional holiday Pops at Christmas, complete with a visit from Saint Nicholas, and at New Year's Eve, during which celebrants and musicians are inundated at midnight with balloons released from Symphony Hall's ceiling.

Not to be forgotten is the fact that the income from perennially popular Pops recordings and the night-after-night sellouts make additionally welcome sounds in the BSO's box office coffers. It may be said that many of the less aware believe the Boston Symphony is the Boston Pops, and the Boston Pops is Arthur Fiedler.

OFF SEASON WITH THE PRINCIPALS

A general trend in 1965 among major American orchestras was to extend their seasons to fifty-two weeks. This led to a significant development in the BSO's growth as an organization. Although it offered as lengthy a season to the majority of its players as any symphonic organization in the United States—its regular season, Pops, and Tanglewood accounting for nearly a year of activity—there was a small but important group of artists whose talents were unprovided for during the Pops season.

Music director Leinsdorf, trustee Henry B. Cabot, Rosario Mazzeo (then personnel manager), and concertmaster Joseph Silverstein formulated the concept of the Boston Symphony Chamber Players (BSCP). It was decided that this group, comprising twelve of the orchestra's first-desk players, would constitute a chamber music ensemble. They would tour with programs of unusual works and carry the Boston Symphony name in an appealing new context. In addition to presenting a challenge to principal artists, the BSCP would be gainfully occupied over a two-month period between the Boston and Tanglewood seasons. Although probably not intentionally, the new concept fulfilled still another of founder Higginson's early thoughts about the BSO: "I would also originate if possible good chamber-concerts . . . they are very charming and peaceful."

The Boston Symphony Chamber Players has proved to be a unique institution. Although numerous chamber ensembles exist elsewhere with circumscribed personnel and repertory, the flexibility of Symphony's chamber organization permits it to explore and present new as well as older works. When required, extra musicians have been brought in from the BSO, and on rare occasions, a guest singer or noted solo instrumentalist has appeared with the BSCP. However, mostly with its own members, it has performed more than three hundred works in its first thirteen years, including many premieres, and has contributed to the expansion of interest in the BSO through its performances and recordings. Contractually, all principal soloists are members of the BSCP. Through this additional responsibility, they maintain an individuality of style and approach essential to their positions as section leaders in the orchestra.

Although the group was formed with the idea that its activities would be confined more or less to the May and June period, the demand for concerts has resulted in appearances within the regular BSO season. In addition to an annual series in Boston, the BSCP appear regularly in New York and environs and elsewhere along the Eastern seaboard. The year after their founding, they made a transcontinental tour of the United States, and in 1967, under government sponsorship, they played in England, the Soviet Union, and West Germany. Concerts are given in connection with the BSO's tours abroad, and in 1972 the group made its South American debut. Its members have performed and given master classes in the Virgin Islands, and have conducted clinics in connection with appearances in many American schools and universities. Now represented on discs playing music from Beethoven to Webern, the first BSCP recording, issued in 1966, won that year's Grammy Award for "Best Chamber Music Performance."

OUT IN THE OPEN AIR

Home for the Boston Symphony is, of course, Symphony Hall. But summer home is Tanglewood, near Lenox in western Massachusetts, where the orchestra has been the centerpiece of the Berkshire Symphonic Festival since 1937. For the orchestra's membership and most of their families, Tanglewood means a wholesale exodus from Boston, lasting from the beginning of July to the end of August. It doesn't mean, however, a vacation from music. On each of eight weekends, three different programs are played on Friday and Saturday evenings and Sunday afternoons. These are prepared in six rehearsals, one of them (on Saturday morning), open to the public. This differs from the Boston schedule, where the same program is rehearsed and repeated for as many as four consecutive subscription performances.

Repetition of works heard in the past Boston season, as well as programming of numerous selections from the standard repertory, has frequently come under fire from the press. However, each Tanglewood summer does offer novelties, a variety of guest conductors and soloists, and occasional series devoted to the works of a single composer. Beethoven weekends are still surefire draws. What must be taken into account is the necessity for balancing the players' workload with the time allotted under Festival conditions.

Most players welcome the annual shift to Tanglewood after an arduous Boston season of symphony and Pops, not only on account of the airy ambience of the surrounding Berkshire Hills (although a few would prefer Tanglewood to be on the Atlantic Ocean), but because it allows for a change in life-style. Despite a continuing active schedule of rehearsals, performances, and in some cases, teaching, there is time for outdoor sports, socializing—no one lives too far from the capacious Shed where concerts take place—and a more relaxed atmosphere for family living. When there are growing children, they are usually intrigued to find summer occupations within the Festival organization as guides, cashiers, or messengers. Older children interested in becoming serious musicians have exceptional opportunities to be auditors, and in some cases participants, in the eight-week swirl of music that fills the Berkshire air.

There is a colony of resolute BSO campers on the shores of Stockbridge Bowl, just down the hill from the Tanglewood grounds.

Some install themselves in tidy summer cottages or board in friendly farmhouses; a few discover rustic shacks in the woods, while a historically minded, ambitious group finds staunch old dwellings waiting to be restored. Gardens are planted, and cold-weather buffs insulate against the winter so that they can return to ski, skate, or toboggan on chance days off from Symphony Hall.

Onstage, for performances, the prescribed dress is warm-weather, country formal. At evening concerts, both men and women wear white jackets, with the appropriate black underpinnings. At afternoon Festival concerts, everyone is dressed in white from top to toe except for black four-in-hand ties for the men. This sightly regimen was upset upon a stifling afternoon in 1936 when none other than the normally "correct" Serge Koussevitzky, as reported by Herbert Kupferberg in his book *Tanglewood*, "asked for—and received—the audience's permission to doff his jacket: 'It is awfully hot. You will escuse if we remove our kowts.'" Listeners, who in those days dressed to the nines even to sit on the lawn, responded positively to the maestro's cue. This precedent-shattering event allowed comfort onstage thereafter, and eventually led to an informality for loungers outside the Shed that Koussevitzky could hardly have envisioned.

Operating simultaneously with the festival are the Berkshire Music Center and Boston University's Tanglewood Institute. The Berkshire Music Center (BMC) provides further training for advanced young musicians while the Tanglewood Institute instructs promising music students of high school age. With Gunther Schuller as artistic director, concertmaster Joseph Silverstein as faculty chairman, and Daniel R. Gustin as administrator, the BMC, headed by Seiji Ozawa, is the continuing realization of a treasured concept of Serge Koussevitzky, who established it in 1940. It is also a realization of an expressed aim of the BSO's founder, Henry Lee

Higginson, who, in a detailed statement of his purposes in establishing a Boston Symphony, wrote:

One more thing should come from this scheme, namely, a good, honest school for musicians. Of course it would cost us some money, which would be well spent. I think that younger musicians, the scholars growing up here, should be taken into the orchestra as a school of training, and should be gradually incorporated into that body, thus supplying fresh and good material—this of course hinging on their quality as musicians, and on their education.

The passage of time, proliferation of young musical talent not only in the Boston area but throughout the world, and the BSO's now-established procedures for joining the orchestra have, of course, modified Higginson's original plan. While this "good, honest school" inspires students and the musicians who oversee them there, the BMC is careful not to become too paternalistic. BMC Fellows come to Tanglewood from far-flung places for eight weeks of concentrated study at the performance level, but it is policy that they should not be "taken from their teachers," Gustin points out. Ozawa, as he further explains, has emphasized that the BMC is not run by the orchestra as a musical "farm team."

In an effort to make the BMC's experience as available as possible to advanced young musicians, its auditions budget has been quadrupled in recent years. Hearings now take place on an international scale under Schuller's direction. All of those invited to the BMC as Fellows have their tuition underwritten, and some assistance is available for travel and housing costs in case of need.

Traditionally, BMC's faculty includes the orchestra's first three violins, the leader of second violins, and first-desk principals of all other sections. Several retired members of the orchestra, and such specialists as BSO violist Eugene Lehner, a former member of the Stradivarius and Kolisch Quartets, librarian Victor Alpert, and musicologist and BSO publications director Michael Steinberg further represent the organization's membership. Assistant personnel manager Harry Shapiro is also the manager of the Berkshire Music Center Orchestra, which operates like a miniature BSO, with its own Players' Committee, rotated seating, and adherence to rehearsal and performance schedules. Discipline is expected to be on a professional level.

In this paraprofessional situation, Gustin explains, the BMC Fellows discover what life in an orchestra is like:

The BSO figuratively "takes its clothes off" so that its faults and virtues are revealed, and before long the kids know everything that goes on. They become exposed to all aspects of professional life—a really wonderful opportunity to learn in concentrated fashion what it is to be an instrumentalist. Conductors can't treat these people other than as pros. They receive the same pressures and the same amenities as if they were in the BSO.

Over a summer, warm relationships develop between Fellows and BSO members. In some cases the friendships continue into the future when many become BSO members themselves. Currently, at least fifty Boston Symphony players previously attended the Center, and it is estimated that almost 10 percent of the membership in this country's major orchestras are former BMC Fellows.

In 1965, the Berkshire Music Center joined with Boston University's School for the Arts to form the Boston University Tanglewood Institute. The Institute offers five summer programs, of which two—ensemble training for high-school-age instrumentalists, and applied music involving individual study and practice—enlist about forty BSO players as faculty, along with some specialists from Boston University. Students, chosen by extensive auditions, are supervised in orchestral and chamber music activities by Symphony musicians, who also give private instrumental lessons.

MUSIC ALONG THE CHARLES

Before Tanglewood, the Boston Symphony's outdoor performances were limited to the city's Charles River Esplanade, a long green strip of land between Beacon Street on one side and the Charles River on the other. A park-like area, it suggested an ideal site for open-air concerts, and in 1929, Arthur Fiedler seized on it as an alfresco extension of Pops. Supported privately, with Fiedler on the podium and an orchestra of mostly BSO colleagues, a series of free warm-weather concerts was launched in a makeshift shell on the Esplanade. Audiences were at first in the 10,000s, growing annually until an all-time record crowd of 400,000 appeared at the U.S. Bicentennial concert on July 4, 1976.

A distinguished alumnus of the Boston Symphony, trumpeter Roger Voisin, found his way into the BSO in the early days of the Esplanade. Son of René Voisin, a trumpeter in the orchestra, and his father's pupil, Roger was commandeered as signal boy to play flourishes on his trumpet to recall Esplanade musicians and audiences at the end of intermissions. So impressed was Fiedler with these miniature performances that he arranged for Roger to audition for the Boston Symphony, which he joined at age seventeen—the youngest player ever to be engaged—and took his place in the trumpet section with his father. Before he retired, Roger Voisin had moved to the first trumpet chair, and since then has been active on the faculty of the Berkshire Music Center and as a judge of Fellowship auditions.

Present at the fiftieth Esplanade celebration in 1978 was John Barwicki, a member of the BSO since 1937, and as a student double bassist, a performer in the first Esplanade concerts in 1929. In response to his comment that "we're the only two left," Fiedler replied, "Come on, John, shall we do it again?" As it is, Barwicki,

Boston-born and -trained, has been playing Pops under Fiedler since joining the orchestra. John, one of the more visibly demonstrative members of the BSO, continues to confirm his involvement with his job. "When I hear something beautiful," he said in a *Real Paper* interview, "I sort of like boil inside, you know, get emotionally upset, and I try to transmit that in my actions." Like Fiedler, Barwicki shows every sign of wanting to keep a good thing going.

There have been a few sour notes in the BSO's alfresco career. During the summers of 1970 and 1971, the Esplanade Orchestra (then comprising mainly BSO players) took part in Boston's "Summerthing" program, which funded a variety of free entertainment all over the city. A mobile shell, programs of the Pops genre, and a genial spirit of informality were greeted by large crowds everywhere, including masses who had perhaps never even heard of or seen Symphony Hall. However, after a stop at the foot of Bunker Hill Monument in Charlestown, a newspaper commentator observed:

Musicians are very sensitive people, particularly dedicated members of famous orchestras. Their musical integrity is riled by inadequate acoustical provisions (mikes weren't in good working order on Wednesday), their pride is wounded by crank hornblowers (a demon was loose behind the shell during the *William Tell* Overture), and they ask why they should suffer capricious lighting and failed sanitary facilities to play for an audience which has even one stone-thrower in it. One musician did concede that "someone should do it, but not the Boston Symphony." [6]

Weather has proved to be a sometime villain as well. The opening Esplanade concert on July 1, 1974, turned out to be only half a concert thanks to a sudden torrential rainstorm. While Beethoven's *Egmont* Overture was being played, ominous thunderclouds were pushing a burning sunset to the horizon on the Cambridge side of the Charles. The sky was darkening overhead at the start

Midnight has arrived at Boston Pops' New Year's Eve celebration in Symphony Hall. Dancing, balloons, confetti, and surprise attractions make this an annual sellout.

(Overleaf) *For fifty years, the alfresco Esplanade Concerts, originated by Arthur Fiedler, have drawn crowds to the banks of the Charles River in the early summer, a record 400,000 having assembled on July 4, 1976.*

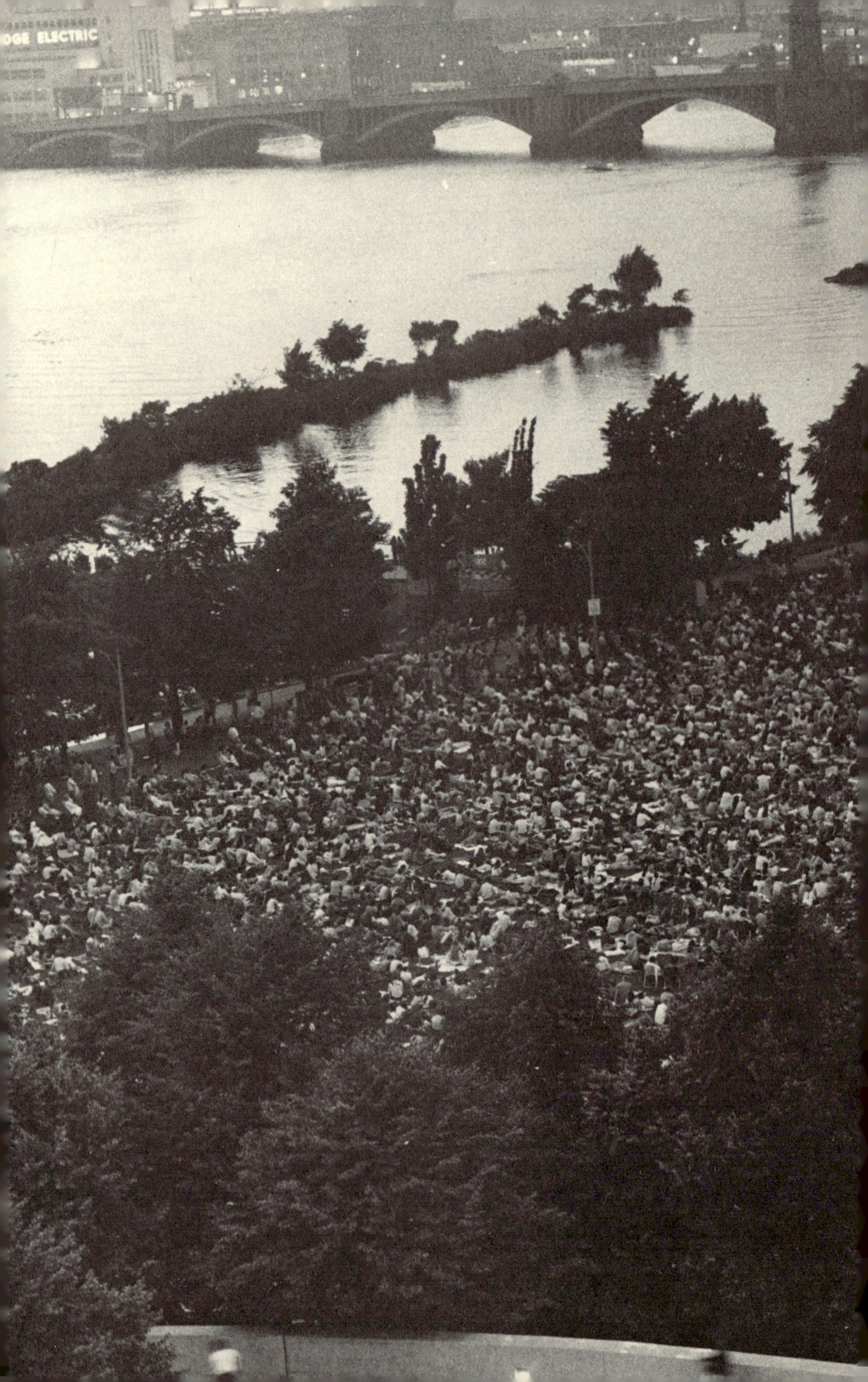
DGE ELECTRIC

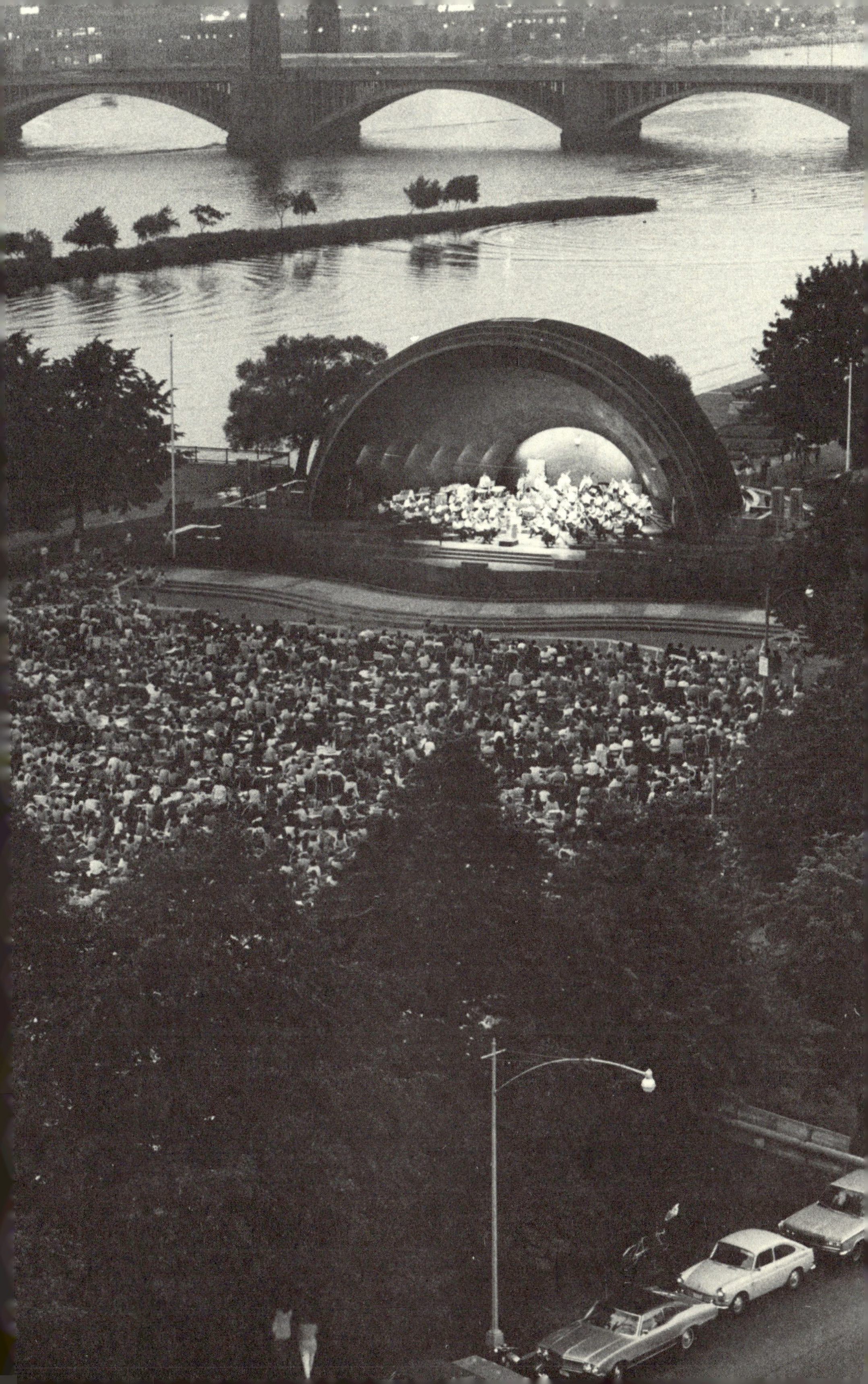

At home, TV director Jordan Whitelaw, with score and performance tapes, assigns spots for the five cameras to be used during a future BSO telecast.

of the *Emperor* Concerto, but conductor Harry Ellis Dickson with Donn-Alexandre Feder on piano began anyway. In the words of a reporter:

When clouds gathered during the playing, warning flashes of lightning lit the horizon, and sudden gusts of wind convulsed the shade trees on the borders of the field, it all somehow seemed to fit in with the titanic sounds from the Shell . . . until the beginnings of a deluge descended. The musicians continued gamely—front row strings listing upstage in their chairs to avoid the rain, Mr. Feder braving it out on slippery keys to the end of the Adagio. But Mr. Dickson finally stopped the music to be greeted with a tumult of cheers and applause rivaling the thunderous blasts from the skies. Then the hopeful vigil began. Blankets and newspapers became temporary tents for many resolute groups on the field. The covered spiral of the Arthur Fiedler Bridge over Storrow Drive sheltered a standing-room-only crowd, and every tree had its covey of refugees. Under the stage of the Shell, orchestra players mopped off their instruments and themselves, in that order, awaiting the word of Mother Nature and the management, in that order, whether the concert would continue.[7]

The rain went on—the concert did not.

On July 4, 1978, however, despite wind and rain that had even prevented the traditional turnaround of "Old Ironsides" in Boston Harbor, Fiedler beat the weather and opened the series for the fiftieth year. This time he conducted the Boston Symphony Esplanade Orchestra, a group which now takes over the playing of summer Pops when the BSO goes to Tanglewood at the beginning of July. There were surprise fireworks, volumes for the maestro containing a half-million congratulatory signatures, and a weatherproofed crowd of 15,000 hardy listeners.

RADIO, TELEVISION, AND RECORDS

The telephone was still in its infancy when the Boston Symphony was founded, but even then there were exploratory attempts to carry the orchestra's concerts, or portions of them, by wire to interested subscribers. Although this means of communication never caught on, it established a precedent for developments many years later which carried the sound and sight of the BSO far beyond Symphony Hall. When the possibilities of broadcasting were first being explored in 1926, a $12,000 gift from Winfield S. Quinby of Brookline made it possible for the orchestra to make its debut on the air with live transmission of its Saturday night concerts, a realization hailed as "the greatest musical triumph in the brief but remarkable history of radio."

In 1951, a series of free educational radio broadcasts on Boston's WGBH was initiated through agreements between the players and management (Charles Munch, Henry B. Cabot, Arthur Fiedler, and manager George Judd), with the blessings of the national and local musicians' union. A permanent installation was placed in Sanders Theater at Harvard to broadcast the BSO Cambridge series, and when these concerts moved to Symphony Hall, the programs continued to be carried live on both Friday afternoons and Saturday evenings. With the establishment in 1958 of the Boston Symphony Transcription Trust, administered by the orchestra, reproductions of BSO radio programs became available worldwide to broadcasting stations. The fees for such reproductions were deposited in the BSO Pension Institution, which had been formed for the benefit of the players in 1903 at the instigation of music director Wilhelm Gericke. In 1959, the BSO made media history when a concert was carried live to Europe for the first time by transatlantic cable.

Jordan M. Whitelaw, who came to Boston station WGBH from Harvard in the early days of FM radio, was first assigned to produce the BSO broadcasts. "This orchestra is extraordinary," he declares. "The goodwill they showed in the beginning has really paid off. All that has happened since—the tremendous TV coverage, as well as the radio broadcasts—has emanated from that 'free' original radio series."

Now a free-lance producer for the BSO's "Evening at Symphony" and "Evening at Pops" series, Whitelaw was first assigned by Channel 2/WGBH to devise a format for telecasting the orchestra's concerts when broadcasting rights were extended to TV in 1957. Although the first concerts were live, later economic factors made it more practicable to tape telecasts, which now are seen on at least one hundred fifty PBS stations around the country. Sponsorship of these programs brings considerable income into the BSO Pension Institution, the happy end result of gracious compliance by the musicians for their own "enlightened self-interest," as Whitelaw defines it.

Thanks to the Whitelaw know-how gained from his long media experience with the BSO, there are no special rehearsals for the telecasts. The programs to be televised are selected well in advance, with the consent of music director Ozawa and manager Thomas Morris. Whitelaw studies scores and recordings, plots camera shots, and in a run-through on the day of taping, places large cards indicating where each instrumentalist will sit and designates to the five or six camera operators a shot-by-shot scenario of each work.

According to Whitelaw:

The musicians do everything possible to cooperate. They never know when they're on camera, but they're constantly aware of being part of the performance. Everyone is proud of the product—they receive comments from their families and viewers from everywhere—and I think I can say that they trust me. Besides, they like the extra money, and there's a certain vanity in having these shows seen all over the country.

In the beginning, there was some concern about the reaction of both musicians and the audience to television lights and cameras in the hall during a concert, but with the use of improved cameras and the latest developments in illumination, the amount of light is cut in half. Nowadays, we almost never have a complaint.

You get what you see, and by now everyone involved is aware of that. Players think in terms of displaying their instruments to best advantage, stagehands also do much to make it look good by clearing empty chairs, etc. And the camera crews—nowhere is there a show like this! Five or six camera mistakes are the exception, and in Haydn's "The Seasons," which adds up to two hours and twenty minutes of music, there was one slip out of 700 shots. It's an amazing accomplishment all around.

Announcer William Pierce, whose measured mellow tones have become a trademark of BSO radio broadcasts and telecasts, began his career in 1952 with the Pops, later taking over the weekly symphony series. When the BSO was carried live on television for the first time, he was the on-the-spot announcer, and as taping became the rule, his announcements were recorded to fit the time specifications of the program. In the case of radio-TV simulcasts, Pierce is responsible for a separate radio narration. From windowed booths on the sides of the Symphony Hall and Tanglewood stages, he has an overhead view of conductor, soloists, and orchestra, and because of his long familiarity with its members and its procedures, Pierce can report the scene (and chance departures from the scheduled script) with authority and, when appropriate, gentle humor.

In its time, the orchestra has taken the opportunity to let its hair down, so to speak, by doing what a well-respected symphonic organization would not be expected to do. At Pops, musicians have donned sporty straw boaters for "Old Timers' Night," double bassists like John Barwicki have spun their instruments around dizzily on pivots to accent the liveliness of a popular selection, and all have weathered a fall of holiday confetti from Symphony Hall's ceiling.

Recording has been an off-and-on part of Boston Symphony musicians' lives since 1917 when the orchestra went en masse to Camden, New Jersey, to make its first record for the Victor Talking Machine Company. Its association with Victor continued until

1938 when its status as a nonunion orchestra collided with new agreements made between the American Federation of Musicians and recording companies, threatening this profitable source of income and exposure for nonmember groups. Thus the need to continue making records was a major factor in the Symphony trustees' final decision to capitulate at long last to unionization of the orchestra in 1942.

Victor's affiliation with the BSO and Boston Pops was resumed in 1942 and continued, an estimated forty million records later, until August 1970 when Deutsche Grammophon Gesellschaft (DGG) became the recording agency. Although Victor in later years had recorded the BSO in Symphony Hall, DGG converted a basement room in the hall for its recording equipment. There the orchestral sound from the auditorium is taped. A basic communication system connects the playback room and the podium—a telephone, and two lights activated from below by the technicians: white for *ready*, red for *play*.

For recording sessions the orchestral musicians find themselves in different circumstances than those of a usual concert. When the stage is used instead of the floor of the hall, it is extended forward to spread the sound and separate the instrumental sections. Onstage, sixteen tracks are used, one for each section and one for a soloist (as in the case of Itzhak Perlman's recording with the BSO of the Stravinsky Violin Concerto in D in February 1978).

Generally, recording sessions are held on nonperformance days for the convenience of musicians and technicians alike. A high degree of concentration is required on everyone's part, particularly since conditions differ markedly from those of a regular performance. Dress is informal, and there is a special effort to avoid extraneous stage noises, unnoticed in concert performances but picked up by electronic equipment. While three hours is the normal allotted time, a four-hour call allows for overage. Playing time, intermissions, and conditions for the use of personnel in recording are designated explicitly in the BSO's Trade Agreement. Minutes are valuable commodities all around.

A typical session often begins with the testing of sound levels by playing sections of the work to be recorded. These are checked by phone with the DGG technicians in the playback room who may ask to hear specific passages involving, say, tuba or timpani. The music director makes certain suggestions for the achievement of balance, readings are indicated and marked, and the first take begins.

When time is called, conductor, soloist, and the appropriate instrumentalists gather downstairs in the playback room where tapes are run, analyzed, and commented upon by the music director, soloist, and the DGG technicians. First-desk musicians and others are there after each take to assess the results, and receive compliments or suggestions about corrections that are deemed necessary in replays. Someone realizes that air conditioning in the hall is affecting the sound and it is shut off. Takes continue and playbacks are minutely examined. DGG officials eye the clock, and finally the session ends thirty seconds after the four-hour call—overtime.

According to Gideon Toeplitz, BSO's assistant manager, the choice of repertory to be recorded depends considerably on the recording company's commitments to other orchestras and conductors, an understandable but limiting circumstance where any symphonic body is concerned. The tremendous growth of interest worldwide in records, and the obvious part that the Boston Symphony has played in its development make its recording affiliations of supreme importance.

THE PLAYERS AND MANAGEMENT

From its beginnings when it was presided over by a beneficent patron, Henry L. Higginson, the Boston Symphony has maintained a close rapport between players and management, and in later years with trustees. When unionization became a fact in 1942, the Corporation (management and trustees) endeavored to make it work in the best way possible, with the result that BSO labor relations have become a model for other orchestras. Negotiations are conducted, as Toeplitz puts it, "with style and a smile." Its Pension Fund is the oldest and one of the best, and its contractual fringe benefits and medical plan compare favorably with those in any industry. As of 1977–1978, basic minimum salary for a Symphony instrumentalist was $25,000 annually.

"By keeping the doors open," assistant personnel manager Harry Shapiro remarks, "management and trustees have made the orchestra feel part of a mutual endeavor. They're available for complaints, and of course there always are some, but for most, the rewards of a fine professional life outbalance the minor irritations."

Such sentiments persist throughout the membership, and concertmaster Joseph Silverstein points out another reason for this long tradition of mutual admiration:

Unlike many other orchestras where management offices are down the street, the library around the corner, and the trustees invisible, we're all under one roof here. Symphony Hall brings us together all the time— it's almost impossible not to know who everyone is. In how many major orchestras would players feel comfortable calling the manager by his first name, and where else is it possible to discuss personal matters with the management?

This long-standing feeling of warmth between the orchestra and the corporation undoubtedly has its roots in the period—over three decades from 1881—when Higginson concerned himself directly with BSO musicians' welfare in general and the individual's own problems in particular. As a lover of music as well as a prosperous business figure, Higginson was a one-man corporation in himself. Fortunately, from the orchestra's formation, he had as its first manager Charles A. Ellis, a man of great experience in musical matters and knowledge of dealing fairly and affably with artists.

He was one whom Higginson could entrust with contractual matters at home and abroad in the engagement of musicians, and his tenure (1881–1918), which coincided with the founder's active involvement, saw the growth and fulfillment beyond the wildest hopes of Higginson's original concept.

According to H. Earle Johnson, when Ellis "was once offered the directorship of the Metropolitan Opera at a salary just fifteen times his current rate," Higginson's reaction was " 'Charlie, I can't run the orchestra without you,' and 'Charlie' stayed." Of Ellis, critic Olin Downes wrote: "Traditions of simplicity, honor, courtliness, hospitality, were typical of his breeding and generation. His conception of power was that of responsibility."

Succeeding Ellis in 1918 was his assistant, William H. Brennan, whose association with Ellis's outside management enterprises, including the tours of Sembrich, Melba, Farrar, and Schumann-Heink, had begun in 1911. Joining Brennan as assistant manager was George E. Judd, who had also worked closely with Ellis, and who, when he in turn succeeded Brennan in 1934, began a term as manager which was to encompass twenty years.

At the beginning of his managership, Brennan faced a changed situation in the BSO. Higginson had turned over its direction to a group of nine trustees, who immediately moved to incorporate. Karl Muck, its music director, had been interned as an enemy alien in March 1918, following an unprecedented furor in the press, while a majority of the German musicians in the orchestra were similarly designated and prevented from performing. A new conductor and replacement instrumentalists had to be engaged hurriedly to be ready for the 1918–1919 season, which, to compound the difficulties, was postponed for two weeks because of an influenza epidemic in Boston. However, open it did, on October 25, with an interim conductor, Pierre Monteux, in charge, pending the delayed arrival from France of the new director, Henri Rabaud. Thus on Monteux had fallen the responsibility of choosing competent new musicians, whom Brennan then contracted. Both Brennan and Judd survived this baptism of fire, according to M. A. DeWolfe Howe, with "judgment, resourcefulness, and alertness."

Rabaud remained for only one season, and Monteux was re-engaged for a five-year term to replace him. Then in 1920 came the new management's second crisis—the first musicians' strike in BSO history. While the impasse essentially was between players demanding higher pay and trustees declaring themselves unable to provide it, manager and conductor were caught in the middle. Once again, more than thirty musicians departed, and once again Monteux and manager Brennan were faced with the necessity of rebuilding the orchestra. When the 1920–1921 season began, virtually a full personnel had been assembled, thanks to the arduous efforts of Monteux and Brennan.

George Judd succeeded to the position of manager ten years into the regime of Serge Koussevitzky (1934) and remained for five years under Koussevitzky's successor, Charles Munch, until 1954. A soft-spoken patrician gentleman who carried on the Higginson and Ellis tradition of straightforward dealing with the players, Judd was the temperamental opposite of the flamboyant Koussevitzky whose relations with his musicians ran hot and cold. Speaking of Judd, Arthur Judson, then manager of the New York Philharmonic, said: "There are some people who devote their time and thought to the job in hand and leave the talking to others. George Judd is one of these." [8]

In the Judd regime there occurred events of major importance to the course the BSO was to take: the negotiations which resulted in the orchestra becoming the established body in the Berkshire Symphonic Festival at Tanglewood in 1936, thus extending the musicians' playing year; and the tenuous situations which led in 1942 to the unionization of the BSO. In the latter imbroglio, the manager again found himself between the contending parties—the BSO's trustees and the American Federation of Musicians, headed by James C. Petrillo. When the issue was finally resolved, it became Judd's task to renegotiate agreements with recording and broadcasting companies under the new conditions, and to supervise the operation of the orchestra's activities in accordance with union regulations. This was not always made easy by Koussevitzky who, although originally a proponent of unionization, often found it hampering to his unique views toward rehearsing and musicians' relations when it became a reality. More than once, Judd was the voice of reason reconciling the angry maestro and a defiant player in passing storms that accompanied adjustment on both sides to a changed relationship.

When George Judd retired in 1954, his parting advice to Thomas D. Perry, Jr., previously his assistant and now his successor, was "Take good care of the BSO." Having learned by observation, Perry could well appreciate the scope of his inheritance. A Yale graduate, with some experience in management before he joined the BSO in 1946, Tod Perry maintained the reputation for fair and harmonious dealing with orchestral affairs that had been a Judd hallmark. While he strived to maintain that delicate balance between trustees and conductors (not always appreciated by the latter) that managers are heir to, players were soon to learn that they could come to him with their personnel or private problems, for advice, or at least for a sympathetic ear.

Although the BSO's first tour abroad took place in 1952 during the Judd tenure, Perry was at the helm when the orchestra returned to Europe (including the Soviet Union) in 1956, and in 1971 and 1976. An eight-week trip in 1960 to the Far East was followed in 1963 by a trans-American tour and in 1969 by a swing through the southern United States. In 1978, the three-week Japanese tour was a responsibility shared by Perry, now the BSO's executive director, with Thomas D. Morris, appointed manager in 1973. Following the 1978 Tanglewood season, Perry retired after twenty-four years as manager/executive director, and in the September following was elected to the orchestra's board of trustees.

When Morris became general manager (a new title) of the Boston Symphony in the fall of 1978, he was at thirty-four the youngest administrator of a major symphony in the United States. Engaged in 1969 to work in the BSO's payroll office, he came with background as a music major (percussion) at Princeton University, a graduate degree from Wharton School of Finance and Commerce, and two years' experience as a managerial intern on a Ford Foundation grant with the Cincinnati Symphony. Within the next few years in Boston, he was made assistant treasurer, then assistant manager, occasionally joining the orchestra as an extra or substitute percussionist.

Upon assuming the managership in 1978, Morris outlined plans for the BSO's second century of operations which starts in 1981. Depending on whether 15.7 million dollars is raised in a Centennial campaign, his plans include such possibilities as: increasing the number of orchestra members in an effort to ease the workload; a program of chamber music to be presented by various ensembles drawn from within the BSO; rehabilitation of and addition to existing facilities at Tanglewood; extension of the orchestra's tours abroad; and added emphasis on the variety of music played and the quality of soloists engaged.

From the beginning, managers' responsibilities have included: the contracting of musicians chosen for the orchestra; implementation of the music director's seasonal programmatic plans; engagement of soloists; overall choice and supervision of administrative personnel; liaison between trustees and musicians, including the music director; representation of the Corporation in union negotiations (since 1942); planning of tours; developing new projects for the growth of the orchestra; lending an ear to questioning players and in-house personnel; and otherwise doing whatever feasible to keep everyone happy.

On the musicians' side, a further aid to smooth relations with the management has been the formation of a number of committees, encouraged by the Corporation, and confirmed by the Trade Agreement. These groups, consisting of players elected for specified terms by the orchestra membership, serve as clearinghouses for matters of mutual concern. Fortunately they have not had occasion to be "watchdog" groups as much as indicators of general feeling within the playing body. The committees—Players', Artistic Advisory, Steering, Dismissal, Rotation, String, and Woodwind—all have specialized functions as their names indicate. "The committees are terrific," personnel manager Moyer declares. "Mostly the members have a deep and healthy love of the orchestra, and they're conscious of being included in decision making for the future."

Probably the most active committee is the Players' Committee, consisting of five musicians elected each year by the orchestra membership and authorized to represent them in negotiations with the management and in interpretation of the existing Trade Agreement. Cellist Robert Ripley who has been chairman four times and secretary for several terms, and who instigated the BSO's open audition procedure, is philosophical about the demands on members of this group.

You're pulled one hundred ways—everyone has his or her own little gripe. But it's important to realize that you develop pride in the organization if you stay any length of time. People's appreciation comes out in the playing quality, which is kept high by working conditions. That's why any suggestion for improvement can be valuable. For instance, the idea of rotation of players within the string section is an attempt to correct a perennial problem. When someone who has worked hard to get into the orchestra is fixed in a rear seat for years, it's easy to fall into a don't-care attitude. You hear what's around you but there is no sense of the sound of the section, and you feel out of things. With rotation comes a new incentive—and it's also good for separating pairs of loggerheads (they sometimes exist, you know), who have been partners for too long.

As a member of the Players' Committee, and an orchestra representative on the Overseers' Personnel Relations Committee, cellist Carol Procter appreciates how the former group provides access to opinions, how people interpret things, and particularly how societal differences affect their outlook. The newer ad hoc Personnel Relations Committee, which originated within the BSO Board of Overseers, serves a policy advisory function, and represents all staff employed at Symphony Hall. It deals with sensitive issues—affirmative action, encouraging minorities to audition for the orchestra and to participate at other levels—and shows the organization's intentions along progressive lines.

Retired manager Tod Perry has described the concept of the Artistic Advisory Committee as the obvious outcome of having among BSO members an enlightened musical resource:

It would be neglectful not to take advantage of one hundred or more well-trained musicians' concerned interest with quality. The committee is a sounding board for opinions about repertory and soloists—and guest conductors, too. Its members are anxious to do well themselves, so they make pertinent artistic suggestions to make this possible. But they aren't aiming to erode the responsibility of the music director, and they certainly don't want to be stuck with the responsibility for final programmatic choices.

A harder line is expressed by a concerned orchestra instrumentalist:

There has been an important change in the attitude of players toward what they play and with whom. They feel entitled to have a say in the artistic destiny of the orchestra, and the Artistic Advisory Committee indicates in this era a day-to-day evaluation of programming, heavily controlled by the music director. Is whoever and whatever supplied us okay? Many in the orchestra are sophisticated enough not to accept without question what's handed them.

While both the Artistic Advisory and Personnel Relations Committees are ad hoc bodies, not empowered to make final managerial decisions, their suggestions and recommendations are listened to very seriously. Although the intricacy of program-making obviously cannot always permit the inclusion of preferred choices among repertory, guest conductors, and soloists, there is a new awareness of the kind of quality in these areas which encourages the orchestra to play at its best.

The late Charles Munch put in writing in 1955 his reflections on his experience as a conductor:

Everywhere I have admired the spirit and the high ideals of the great orchestras. Each has its own character, its own color, and its own special quality. But the musicians always know that they are only individual cells of a larger body. They know that they are completely dependent on one another and they place their talent at the service of the musical collective of which each is but a part. They teach us an important lesson in human solidarity. It is an honor to conduct them.

During Munch's tenure as the BSO's musical director (1949–1962), certain of the ideas for players' participation in the affairs of the orchestra were beginning to take form. It would have interested him that several decades later these constructive elements have taken new directions in the interests of "human solidarity."

IV
Music Away from Home

From its earliest days the Boston Symphony has taken its music and its musicians outside Boston. In its second season (1882–1883), under Georg Henschel, the BSO crossed the Charles River to inaugurate the Cambridge series at Harvard's Sanders Theater. This series continued for eighty-one years until it was decided that Cantabrigians could cross the river and hear the concerts in more capacious Symphony Hall. The annual series in Providence began in 1883, while runouts to Worcester, Salem, Lynn, Fitchburg, New Bedford, and other rail-connected towns and cities also occurred in BSO's early years.

By the end of his second season as music director, and after a strenuous year of reinstating discipline among the players by insistence on adequate rehearsals, Wilhelm Gericke felt confident that the orchestra was ready to be heard farther afield. In 1886, neither Philadelphia nor Chicago had permanent symphonic organizations, and it was in Philadelphia that heartening recognition occurred, far away from home, stimulating BSO members and their advocates in Boston. Gericke, quoted in M. A. DeWolfe Howe's history, *The Boston Symphony, 1881–1931*, says:

> The end of the second season, however, brought a great change. We made our first tournee to different cities, and at this time in Philadelphia the Orchestra there earned its first real success. The musicians began to understand what the hard work and earnest study had meant, and what results were reached by it; it opened their eyes and gave them a feeling of pride and satisfaction with themselves.

With a certain trepidation, however, Gericke waited a year before introducing the BSO to New York—in 1887 at old Steinway Hall. The delay was mitigated no doubt by the fact that New Yorkers already had their own established Philharmonic Society whose patrons' tastes had been maintained by the high musical standards set by Theodore Thomas, its conductor since 1879. Happily, the visitors' debut was a two-way revelation—for New Yorkers to hear such a surprisingly formidable body of musicians; for the Bostonians to feel that they belonged to a musical organization of the first rank. On this basis, annual visits to New York have continued to this day.

As costly as the early tours were they served not only to establish the reputation of the orchestra in other cities, but in Boston as well. The news of the BSO's acclaim on the road traveled fast back to the players' hometown, and when they returned from a long trip to the Middle West in the spring of 1887, Howe reports of Gericke's reception: "A victorious general, fresh from serving his country, could not have been more rapturously received."

The value of touring having been confirmed to the BSO and its musicians, trips to distant points following the Boston season became standard practice. W. E. Walter, for a number of years the orchestra's publicity representative, gives a colorful account of those early times in an article written in retrospect for *Harper's Weekly* of March 29, 1913. Describing a typical stop on the itinerary, he pictures the conductor pacing the solitary dressing room as he contemplates the evening's program, the musicians "backstage in dust and gloom, placing their celluloid dickies inside of their evening waistcoats" while grumbling about hotels, Pullman sleeping cars, and provincial food. Out front by the box office, "the manager, in expansive white shirt bosom and fur coat [is] extending the glad hand to the music connoisseurs of Medicine Hat."

Lest he be thought to be denigrating the tastes of these "connoisseurs," Walter observed:

What is hard for a conductor to realize is that the average city of the Midwest is usually keener in the matter of programs than cities which possess their own orchestras ... They know what has been played in Boston, New York and Chicago, and let a novelty have success in any of those cities, they are after it hot-foot. So much so that it is becoming the fashion in many of these cities, judging from the newspaper criticisms and the talk in the clubs, to treat the classics with good-natured tolerance, and a generation is growing up that can glibly discuss Debussy, Strauss, Reger, and other ultra-moderns, but doesn't know the "tune" of the first movement of Schubert's *Unfinished Symphony* when they hear it.

Interestingly, the same sentiments were expressed in 1908 in an interview with Karl Muck, then completing his first engagement as BSO music director: "... in the few visits I have made to Western cities," he said, "I found the audiences enthusiastic and discriminative, and the modern works appeared to find as much appreciation as the classics." [1]

Back in the days before substantial guarantees and enlightened sponsorship, the Boston Symphony took to the road with more hope than assurance of making ends meet. In the hands of the manager rested the responsibility for getting conductor and players there and back with a minimum of financial loss and internal combustion problems. Walter, in his article of 1913, expressed an ever-recurring fact of orchestral traveling life:

On these road tours, orchestras feel the high cost of living.... In the glad old, bad old days before the Interstate Commerce Law, the railways waited on orchestra managers and were not parsimonious in their offers of low-priced transport. Now managers wait on railways and call themselves blessed if they can so arrange a tour which will admit of a round-trip rate. In former years, two dollars a day was ample for the maintenance of the man on the road, and some of the thrifty practitioners of the soothing art saved money on it. Now, forsooth, they complain that double that amount barely suffices to keep body and soul together. In the old days they were so glad to get a sleeper on a long jump that the conductor himself did not scorn a section when a drawing room was not to be had. Now it demands the finest diplomacy of a manager to decide who shall have lower berths and who upper. The humble but filling sausage which used to peep from the instrument case of the traveling musician has disappeared, making way for the *ris de veau financière*, served on real china.

Economically "bad times" which delayed the construction of Symphony Hall at the turn of the century also curtailed the orchestra's Western trips for a number of years. They had resumed, however, by the time of Karl Muck's first directorship (1906–1908), and several years after his return to the BSO in 1912, a tour event of major significance took place.

The orchestra's first visit to the West Coast occurred in May 1915 when the Boston Symphony was engaged to be a star attraction of the Panama-Pacific International Exposition in San Francisco. Thirteen concerts were given in an enormous Festival Hall, with Dr. Karl Muck as conductor, and with public and critical reaction bordering on the ecstatic. When it was all over, the San Francisco *Examiner* exclaimed:

Think of it. The $65,000 expended on bringing the Boston Orchestra to the Coast was paid by Monday night and the receipts for the two subsequent concerts are pure gain. That means something like $10,000. Is that not a goodly return to thank Henry Lee Higginson for foregoing his idolized "pops" in order that we of San Francisco might hear what kind of music this greatest orchestra in the world can make? [2]

Musicians, even then becoming used to touring, found themselves playing in a 4000-seat auditorium, altered acoustically by "great folds of felt above the orchestra, and a curtain before the lower part of the organ," apparently to good effect. The crowds were tremendous (except for a three B's program, critically acclaimed, nevertheless), and newspaper headlines like "Bostonians Cast Spell Over First Night Audience" and "Orchestra's Art Flawless in Giant Task" kept public enthusiasm at fever pitch. No wonder. Redfern Mason of the *Examiner* wrote after the opening concert: "People had come from Denver, from Los Angeles, from a hundred places large and small in the Western States, and some had crossed the continent in order to combine the delights of the Exposition and the privilege of hearing the greatest orchestra in the world . . . I do not believe that an audience ever spent a more delightful evening than we San Franciscans did last night." [3]

By the time of Koussevitzky's arrival in 1924, touring was in full swing again. As Howe recalls: "Now the Boston Symphony Orchestra visits a West far different from the hinterland through which Theodore Thomas once campaigned with *Traumerei* and the *Linnet Polka* to keep his orchestra from bankruptcy or the West where Henschel or Gericke would make an occasional springtime venture." Koussevitzky and the players embarked "with genuine eagerness" for concerts in such "musically alert" cities as Chicago, Detroit, Minneapolis, Cleveland, Cincinnati, and Rochester, each of which had "its own splendid orchestra and a seasoned public."

Veterans of some later, preairborne tours, under other conductors, recall with a certain nostalgia the spirit of camaraderie these more leisurely excursions induced. There were practical jokes—the discovery and dilution of a bottle of Scotch, concealed by a violinist to last through the trip; the birth of a subsequent tour catch-phrase—"Here, Fifi!"—intoned by the maestro's wife as she walked her dog on railroad sidings en route, outside cars where musicians were playing poker or trying to catch forty winks.

Air travel, however, has largely eliminated such innocent diversions since the orchestra often finds itself at its destination before time becomes a burden. Even the fourteen-hour flight to Japan in 1978, with a brief stop in Anchorage, Alaska, was lessened by study of guidebooks, attempts to master a few useful phrases, consumption of food and drink Oriental style, sleep, or the viewing of a pictorially intriguing yet incomprehensible Tokyo-made film. The European trips, first made with the orchestra personnel divided between two planes, now waft everyone abroad in one giant airliner. Musicians' trunks and instrument boxes, of course, go on separate cargo carriers.

When the Boston Symphony made its European debut in 1952 under the batons of Charles Munch and Pierre Monteux, Paris was the first stop for a festival, "Masterpieces of the Twentieth Century," arranged by the Congress for Cultural Freedom. After a gala concert at the Paris Opera in a program of works by Samuel Barber, Walter Piston, Roussel, Honegger, Debussy, and Ravel, conducted by Munch, the reaction, according to Boston critic Cyrus Durgin, was "one ovation after another." The next concert, at the Théatre des Champs-Elysées, was an occasion of another sort—Pierre Monteux conducted the BSO in Stravinsky's *Sacre du Printemps*, which in 1913 in the same place had provoked a riot. This time, however, the reception was tumultuous in its favor. Two Symphony players—Louis Speyer, English horn, and Henri Girard, double bass, had participated with Monteux in the 1913 performance. According to Durgin, Speyer attributed the scandal not so much to the music as to the "poor" Nijinsky choreography and the hideous costuming of the dancers—"enough to make one sick." Abdon Laus, later a bassoonist with the BSO, had been a player on that noisy evening, and had a sympathetically autographed photo of Stravinsky to prove it.

Another stop on their tour was a concert at The Hague, with Queen Juliana in attendance. After the concert she received not only conductor Munch and manager Judd, but the two Dutch-born, thirty-year-plus veteran members of the BSO—bassoonist Boaz Piller and cellist Jacopus Langendoen.

At the Frankfurt concert, there was a proxy tribute to violinist Daniel Kuntz, who had been an original member of the BSO in 1881 and remained until 1914. Aged ninety-two at tour time but remaining in Boston, Kuntz was remembered by a parchment-bound greeting folder which contained a picture of himself as a young man, violin in hand, a view of his native town, Oberstaufenbach, and "an illuminated message," signed by the burgomeister and other dignitaries. Accepted by manager Judd, it was delivered to Kuntz at the tour's end.

Not all of the tour stops were in major cities, however. Metz in Alsace-Lorraine was described by critic Durgin as the most eager to please, with the least facilities. Having no concert hall, the Salle des Mines, a spacious dance hall, was converted for the concert by building a carpeted stage large enough for the BSO's one hundred players and decorating it with a garden of potted palms, topped by a large American flag. The reception which followed produced not only a feast of unparalleled local cuisine, but a rare conjoining of musicians with an audience of Alsatians and Lorrains, people who have had a history of maintaining a cool political and sociological distance between themselves under ordinary circumstances.

The Boston Symphony returned to Europe in 1956 when the

orchestra became the first American symphonic organization to concertize in the Soviet Union. Munch also led a first BSO tour of the Far East in 1960, the eight-week itinerary including appearances in Japan, the Philippines, Okinawa, Taiwan, Australia, and New Zealand. The second transpacific trip, in 1978, under Seiji Ozawa's direction, was confined to thirteen concerts in three weeks in Japan. There were three-week returns to Europe, in 1971 under William Steinberg and Michael Tilson Thomas (during which Arthur Fiedler and the Boston Pops made their transoceanic debut), and in 1976 under Ozawa. (Visits to China and to music festivals abroad are projected for 1979, with a cross-country Centennial celebration planned for 1980–1981.)

Wuppertal, a many-leveled site not far from Düsseldorf, played host to the Boston Symphony in 1971. An industrial city dating back to the eleventh century, it keeps an opera house and a dramatic repertory theater running ten months a year, maintains a "Schwimmoper" for a prestigious export—Olympic swimmers—and boasts a zoo, a famed Clock Museum, and an art gallery (Manet to Dali, Rodin to Giacometti). Michael Tilson Thomas conducted Debussy, Beethoven, Schoenberg (*Five Pieces*), Mozart (Sherman Walt rapturously received in the bassoon concerto), and Ravel's *La Valse* for a Symphony Hall-like audience in the comfortable, rectangular, crème and terra-cotta Stadthall. This hall, according to one listener, has "the kind of reception that gladdens artists' hearts."

In 1976, during another European visit, the BSO played in Linz, Austria, for which town Mozart wrote a symphony, and, according to Richard Dyer, has "a fattening nut cake named after it." While it didn't look like a cosmopolitan musical center, Dyer wrote in the Boston *Globe:* "In some ways this may be the most significant triumph of the current European tour. For once, the hall was not filled with the city's self-congratulatory American and corporate colonies; these were Austrian people who go to concerts because they like to—and they are used to important music-making."

In many of the most recent overseas tours, corporate sponsorship has been an important factor. While growing awareness of the natural link between commercial and performing arts organizations has been a gradual achievement, a number of American business institutions active in foreign countries have realized the wisdom of assisting in the export of such a prestigious native cultural product as the Boston Symphony. In 1971, three Massachusetts companies with offices in Europe—the Gillette Company, the Massachusetts Port Authority, and Stanley Home Products—became, along with Deutsche Grammophon Gesellschaft (the BSO's recording agency), sponsors of the orchestra's thirteen concerts in six countries. The next European trip, in 1976, was made possible by the International Program of Colgate-Palmolive, while the orchestra's three-week, thirteen-concert tour of Japan in 1978 was courtesy of a grant from the Coca-Cola (Japan) Company, Ltd., who, like previous sponsors, saw to it that musicians, Friends, and the press were handsomely entertained by resident representatives along the way.

Touring has thus become an accepted fact of Boston Symphony musicians' lives, albeit with varying degrees of enthusiasm. "I love to travel," says violist Earl Hedberg, who joined the orchestra for its second European trip in 1956. "Where do we go next?" On the other hand, bassist John Salkowski, who spends his vacation time away from the BSO as group travel director of "Journey to Music," an annually organized tour of opera houses and concert halls in Europe and behind the Iron Curtain, prefers being a listener to performing when away from home. "In unfamiliar places, it's a relief to leave the tensions of performing to others," he feels.

Some people with families begrudge time away, but others like the idea of bringing their mates along for a chance to see the world beyond Symphony Hall. For the wife of one violinist "it is the best life imaginable—the opportunity to travel with music and musicians. But it disturbs me that some read or sleep and don't even look out the windows to see so many wonderful things."

Actually, touring abroad in the jet age, as exemplified by the BSO's 1978 trip to Japan, is made as nearly painless as possible for the travelers. The result of several years of meticulous planning by the management, and execution principally under the tour direction of assistant manager Gideon Toeplitz and transportation manager Harry Shapiro, the two-way flight across the Pacific and the progress by bullet-train or bus between each of nine Japanese cities worked with astonishing precision. Weighty personal luggage was collected before departure and reappeared in one's next assigned hotel room. Upon arrival at each new stop, members picked up their room keys which were waiting in alphabetized envelopes. Slips distributed in advance to everyone bore assigned car and seat numbers for rapid boarding of the Japanese trains, which do not wait for laggards.

The chance of lost luggage was minimized by the provision of an individualized travel number, tags, and BSO stickers in quantity. Everyone received a pocket-sized, day-by-day tour book, listing hotels, halls, scheduled arrival-and-departure and concert times, along with currency, climate, customs, and such surprising indigenous information as "tipping is not expected." What a different kind of trip that 1886 excursion to Philadelphia and Chicago must have been!

Perhaps as a result of the first extensive (and exhausting) eight-week tour of the Far East in 1960, the players' Trade Agreement with the Boston Symphony Corporation now spells out very specifically the terms for acceptance by the orchestra membership of projected trips. Any scheduled travel of more than twenty-five days must be announced to the musicians for a majority vote of approval, which vote shall be binding upon the whole orchestra.

Number of services, per diem allowances, free days, and mode of lodging and transportation are similarly defined.

On a tour or a runout, each orchestral musician shares space with three others in a personal "trunk," a battleship-gray wooden box which is an instrument case and a container for concert clothes and other performance essentials; it is not a container for foreign purchases or overflow from personal luggage. "All trunks must weigh the same on arrival back in the United States as they did on departure," admonishes the players' travel handbook. The trunk is the instrumentalist's home away from home. It is an unprivate dressing room in whatever backstage space alien halls may provide, but its convenience just a few steps from the platform allows players to be transformed instantly after the concert into eaters, sleepers, sightseers, or whatever life on the road may offer. Everyone has his own key to the padlock that locks it, but Al Robison, the BSO stage manager who supervises the hefty crews that move the trunks from hall to hall, has a monster ring of duplicates to these holy of holies, since even the most alert traveler has been known to misplace this vital laissez-passer.

On one European tour, a musician arrived at the border control between Spain and France only to realize that he had inadvertently left his passport in the concert clothes he had worn the night before. Packed in the trunk, it was on its way in a separate plane to Paris. A driver's license, backed by the reputation of the BSO, persuaded stern officials on both sides of the barrier to let him pass. It was a greatly relieved instrumentalist who rejoined his travel permit backstage at the Palais de Chaillot the next night.

Safe passage for such invaluable baggage overseas and on land is one of the many responsibilities Alfred Robison has inherited. Having joined the BSO staff in 1951, he has learned to be ready for any emergency. A first priority is the prompt arrival of the instruments. A scale drawing for the proper disposition of twenty-five wardrobe trunks and instrument boxes, plus such miscellaneous items as a traveling podium and music desk, in a forty-foot trailer, twelve feet four inches to thirteen feet four inches high, is the tried and true solution for touring in the United States. Abroad, where trucks may be sixty feet long but not so high, certain adjustments obviously must be made. As for transoceanic trips, cargo dimensions differ with airlines and plane types, so new ways are found to solve this three-dimensional puzzle. "I've fitted them into everything but canoes," Robison observes.

On a pre-Robison European tour, the orchestra's first, in 1952, the late critic Cyrus Durgin, who accompanied the BSO on behalf of the Boston *Globe*, reported an unavoidable delay encountered by one of two trucks carrying vital equipment from Bordeaux to Paris, there to connect with the Calais boat train for England, the trip's last stop. One truck made it on time, but the other was immobilized by a crowd awaiting the start of an overnight bicycle race from Bordeaux to Paris. Truck Number 2 missed the train and the boat, with the result that wardrobe trunks, six double basses, and boxes of music arrived at Royal Festival Hall in London just before 8:00 P.M. Musicians and audience took it in stride, according to Durgin, and the concert which started one hour late was greeted by a capacity house with rousing cheers.

Considering that on foreign trips, more than four tons of equipment, along with 200 people must be moved from place to place on a split-second timetable, the results have been extraordinary. Only once during Robison's tenure have instruments failed to arrive on time—in 1956 when the trailer-truck was held up for inspection behind the Iron Curtain, in Czechoslovakia, following the Soviet Union concerts. "Somehow a Canadian doctor bailed us out," Robison recalled, "and when I phoned Vienna to let them know we were finally on our way [manager] Tod Perry said, 'We'll begin with the intermission—full speed ahead.'"

(Top) *A deserted corner of an airport lounge finds trumpeter Rolf Smedvig, with his instrument muted, turning waiting time into practice time.*

(Bottom) *A parterre box in Vienna's gilded Musikvereinsaal furnished violinist Cecylia Arzewski with a suitable warm-up place before tour rehearsal.*

(Top left) *First violist Burton Fine, "shoeless in Amsterdam," chooses the informality of his hotel room to "warm up the digits" before leaving to perform.*

(Top right) *A musician's home away from home is his wardrobe trunk, set up in backstage corridors on tour. Here violinist Gerald Gelbloom slips into concert clothes before a performance in a European hall.*

(Right) *A hotel room with a view and a phone directory to practice on serve percussionist Arthur Press when away from the concert hall.*

A fourth-generation representative of a show business family, Robison served his apprenticeship backstage in theater, opera, and ballet, and when the BSO beckoned, his father said, "Get in there and tell them yes, I can do anything. You'll like it." Al accepted his dad's advice, and subsequently trained an ear on all that happens on the concert platform, as well as an eye on the needs of his "boys and girls." Since he supervises and assists in arranging the orchestra seating onstage for each number, both in Symphony Hall and in tour houses at home and abroad, his logistic and musical know-how are constantly brought into play.

New additions to the repertory call for special measures. In Boston, where its world premiere was the second number on the program, Barbara Kolb's *Soundings,* requiring an unusual seating arrangement, was adapted to the wishes of the composer and conductor Ozawa. "Nobody wants to watch us put on a show," Robison said, "so we set the stage in the shortest possible time. On tour in Japan, however, the Kolb piece opened the program, so the stage could be preset, and with Miss Kolb's help we were able to arrange things more closely to her specifications."

As stage manager, Robison is just offstage with a towel for brow mopping or a glass of mineral water when conductor or soloist comes off dripping after a strenuous number. Near at hand are smelling salts, Band-Aids, and other emergency measures for anyone temporarily overcome in the strenuous onstage battle of music. Thanks to Robison's backstage ministrations, the BSO, like Shakespeare's snail, travels "with its house on its head," and the members, on the platform at least, are very much at home in whatever foreign land. And no wonder, considering Robison's unabashed devotion to Symphony Hall and its denizens: "I just happen to love this place," he declares.

Another vital personage on the BSO's foreign tours since 1956 has been the orchestra's eminent official physician, Dr. Keran

Chobanian, who is present at all concerts and on call for emergencies in the course of the trip. Not only does he provide the travelers with advance preventive advice about dressing for the climate to be encountered, inoculations required by each country, and personal remedies to include in one's luggage, but he is on hand to minister when the unforeseen strikes. Dr. Chobanian will not soon forget a twenty-four-hour period (fortunately a nonperformance day) during the 1978 Japanese tour when mass reaction to a local shellfish delicacy served at a party for the players brought him ninety-two distress calls—almost simultaneously. Chills and high fever were only some of the sudden symptoms, but by concert time the next night in Osaka, the epidemic had subsided, and players and doctor completed the itinerary without further spectacular incidents.

The presence of women as members of the orchestra at first raised certain new social problems on the road. Louise Came, the first of her sex to be under a BSO season contract, played second harp during 1937–1938. When the first runout to Providence was scheduled, she wondered what she should do about changing for the concert, since she obviously could not use her harp case as an offstage dressing room, in company with all-male colleagues. The solution was to don her long black velvet dress with white fur trimmings in Boston, and ride the train with the orchestra men to Providence. There, she was given safe passage on the brief walk from station to theater by a gallant flutist (who years later was to become her husband), James Pappoutsakis, who also saw her to the train for the return trip to Boston.

When Carol Procter joined the BSO cello section in 1965, fresh from New England Conservatory and a summer at Tanglewood's Berkshire Music Center, she encountered marked solicitude from her many "professional fathers." In anticipation of the orchestra's upcoming visit to New York, Rosario Mazzeo, then personnel manager, gently advised that she "stay with friends, rather than in a hotel with all those men."

Nowadays, the orchestra's female contingent, numbering eleven at latest count, tours without benefit of any special concessions. As at Symphony Hall, a special women's dressing room is always provided backstage in halls from London to Tokyo, and individually they have endured such indignities of the road as a memorably infested Russian hotel room or a tainted Oriental oyster with an equanimity sometimes surpassing that of some of their male fellow trippers.

"On tour," one lady musician observes,

we're all like sheep herded together, male and female, getting to know one another socially as opposed to being business colleagues. We're all relaxed, free of family and home responsibilities, and we can react agreeably and naturally. It took a while for the men to get used to female fellow travelers. They were hesitant to include us on sightseeing trips to the night spots or the slums, but with their able assistance, we learned how to handle ourselves, and eventually we all became outgoing, supportive tourists together. Like all large, cliquish organizations, one finds whom to go with—those whose interests are on similar wavelengths. Everyone's used to women on tour now, but the men are still pleasantly gallant and slightly protective, and we can't say we object to that.

Men and women together, particularly the younger members on their first tours abroad with the BSO, take advantage of sights to be seen. In 1971, the orchestra had a conducted tour through the Hanover plant of Deutsche Grammophon to witness the process of record taping, pressing, and packaging. In 1978 in Japan, they watched the weaving of cloth for the traditional *obi*, and paid a few yen at a traditional shrine for fortunes printed on wisps of paper, attaching them to tree branches in the temple gardens to be wafted away if they weren't favorable. Over the years, the BSO has penetrated the Berlin Wall, sailed on the Danube, climbed the Eiffel Tower, explored the Ginza, visited the birthplace of Beethoven and the homeplace of Bruckner, and otherwise enriched their playing with the experiences new and old sights in the world have to offer.

Musicians seem more interested in reading reviews on tour than at home where the critics are known quantities. There is usually a rush for the morning-after newspapers, no matter in what language, followed by a search among their colleagues for a qualified translator. In many places abroad, however, there is not the great urgency to put critiques immediately into print that has become traditional in the United States, with the result that reviews often follow the orchestra to its next stop via the BSO press representative.

The critic of the *Christian Science Monitor*, traveling with the BSO in 1971, recalled a scene in a Hamburg hotel lobby:

One musician was in the course of translating a morning-after review headed "A Virtuoso Sits At Every Desk," and read in satisfaction to the end. Then he pondered the headline, and his brow clouded: "But he doesn't say which one of us it is," thereby adding to the inside "joke-lore" of orchestras where two players share each stand.

London, having five orchestras of its own and an unquenchable national pride, tends to treat visiting groups with a certain condescension which reached its nadir in 1971 when one anguished aisle-sitter "with reluctance... stayed to the end." On the Continent, however, where reviewers are not above taking potshots at local institutions, one could have read that same year in Berlin, "Too bad that Herr von Karajan was not there to hear that [Beethoven's Fifth]," and in Vienna, "This orchestra shows that in Boston at least the musicians do not play like machines." In Richard Dyer's Boston *Globe* report of the 1976 trip, he found London more receptive, *The Times* waxing poetic of the BSO's Brahms as "red in tooth and claw..." while this time the Viennese press seemed to concentrate its mix of kudos and darts on conductor Seiji Ozawa.

During the Japan tour of 1978, under Ozawa, there was also an understandable display of national pride. Katsuo Matsumoto, writing in the *Yomiuri Shinbun*, asked: "What new interpretation of the giant Mahler Symphony would Ozawa bring to us? We cannot answer, but I imagined during the concert that the performance was like a clay figure having life breathed into it. I could see the miracle of music becoming alive. This was because of Ozawa, a Japanese conductor. It was really strange that suddenly I had a patriotic feeling." As for an unknown work: "The Kolb *Soundings* is a good example of the new Boston Symphony style. The piece is by an American composer. It's very sensitive music and the Japanese audience liked it unexpectedly. This music is not far from the world of Mitsuru Takechi. Only Ozawa could find out the similarity between the two."

The chief music critic of *Asahi Shinbun*, Yoshida Hidekazu, echoed his colleague's enthusiasm for Ozawa: "How wonderful a conductor he is now! It is inevitable that musicians and audiences all over the world admire and love him . . . I was very glad to hear the Boston Symphony in such good shape. The entire orchestra was calm and composed. Every section, the brass, woodwinds, and strings, in particular, created a beautiful sound." Shafi Al Hoseini, in the *Mainichi Daily News,* had obviously done his homework: " 'To play the best music in the best way,' the hope of the orchestra's founder expressed almost 100 years ago, was realized in full." [4]

Touring having become a predictable way of life for orchestra players, its demands have generated a variety of responses. One man gathers his old clothes and packs them for everyday use, discarding articles as the tour progresses. The wife of another player assembles her husband's wardrobe, assigning the essentials for each day to a separate plastic bag. Some travel with an impressive supply of such health foods as nuts and raisins, while there are those who have a list, researched in advance or familiar from past experience, of vegetarian and dairy restaurants and shops in each tour city.

Many musicians are inveterate shoppers, a tendency which burgeons when their spouses are on the trip. "We still haven't found places to put what we picked up last time," one player observed resignedly. Word of rare finds spreads rapidly, and bargains prove hard to resist. Occasionally, the bulky purchase which proved irresistible at the first tour stop has dimmed appreciably as new tempting attractions appear along the itinerary's route.

For collectors, spare time on tour can be a field day. In Kyoto, English hornist Laurence Thorstenberg acquired a thirteenth-century, incense-darkened temple Buddha to add to his other treasures of wood-carved primitive art. Probably the most sizable acquisition was made by timpanist Vic Firth, a car buff and member of the American Rolls Royce Club, who bought a 1967 Rolls Royce "Corniche" while on a European trip and had it sent home, though not in his tour luggage. Prints from Japan, modern paintings from Europe, furniture and fabrics from everywhere, joined by cameras, computers, watches, and jewelry find their way back to Boston with each tour.

Museum and theater buffs seek out familiar and new sites to explore, while trombonist Gordon Hallberg, a championship bicycle racer, even found a bicycle course in Tokyo. For violinist Leonard Moss, an avid bird watcher, leafy foreign parks and placid lakesides are invitations to bring out his binoculars, while for most string players, there is a favorite luthier to be visited in each city. Richard Plaster, contrabassoonist and a student of Oriental languages, put his knowledge into practice during the Japanese engagement, as did native-born violinist Ikuko Mizuno, whose services as translator, geographical, historical, and gustatory authority were eagerly sought and graciously delivered.

For violinist Bo Youp Hwang, a native of Korea, who had furthered his studies and embarked on a professional career in the United States, the BSO's visit to the Far East permitted a first family reunion in many years. For two violinists, Ronald Knudsen and Sheldon Rotenberg, and cellist Carol Procter, who participated in the cultural exchange program between the Japan Philharmonic and the Boston Symphony, the trip provided a reunion with friends and a renewal of interests acquired during that provocative musical bows-across-the-sea program, now unfortunately lapsed for economic reasons. For French horn player Richard Mackey, it was a return to Tokyo where he had been a principal for several years with the Japan Philharmonic before joining the BSO.

On the 1978 trip to the Far East, as on the European tours in 1971 and 1976, the orchestra was accompanied by groups of well-wishers from the board of trustees (including its chairman, Talcott M. Banks), and the board of overseers, as well as from the BSO's Friends organizations.

The formation of the Friends of the Boston Symphony was the brainchild of Edward A. Taft, a BSO trustee, who envisioned a continuing organization of contributing supporters that would provide a substantial source of income against the orchestra's annual deficit. In its first year, 1934, there were 697 Friends, and with Mr. Taft as the first chairman, membership increased until in 1978–1979 there were over 7000 in all. This number included a related group, Friends of Music at Tanglewood, formed later to include BSO supporters in the Berkshire Hills area.

Friends' tour chairmen—Mrs. Harris Fahnestock and Mrs. Stephen V. C. Morris (Europe), and Mrs. Thomas Gardiner (Japan)—spent months of advance planning for unusual events to supplement the itineraries of nonperforming travelers. In addition to attending BSO concerts and receptions given for the musicians by government officials and corporate tour sponsors, the Friends have been cocktail guests at the House of Lords, attended opera in Germany, Austria, and Italy, been conveyed down the Elbe on a German naval corvette, lunched at Maxim's, attended a Jean Patou fashion show, and in Japan, witnessed the *chanoyu* (tea ceremony), and *ikebana* (art of flower arranging), and visited Beppu's hot springs, the Marine Palace at Oita City, and the botanical gardens at Chinoike Jigoku.

A memorable experience shared by BSO players and Friends, as a prelude to the final concert in Paris in 1971, was provided by Admiral Schweitzer and his pianist wife, Nicole Henriot-Schweitzer, who invited them to visit Basse la Futaie, home of the late Charles Munch, at Louveciennes outside the city. There they were conducted through the large, rambling house, filled with souvenirs of Munch's career, and treated to an elaborate outdoor buffet on the ample green lawns, where they were joined by members of two other Munch orchestras, the Orchestre de Paris and the Orchestre Nationale. Needless to say, talk of the man with whom so many of the Bostonians had worked, and of music in general, served as the common denominator for an extraordinary occasion tacitly presided over by a much admired maestro, gone but not forgotten.

Munch was spectacularly honored during the BSO's 1976 visit to Paris, where the last performance of the tour, conducted by Seiji Ozawa, was a tribute to his former mentor, fondly remembered by many musicians still in the orchestra. Before an audience of five thousand in the Palais des Congrès, the Berlioz *Requiem* was presented, with the Boston Symphony joined by the Orchestre de Paris, the Garde Républicaine band (which had contributed several valuable members to the BSO in 1918), and the choruses of the Paris Opera and l'Orfeon Donostiarra. "At the end of his seventh and last curtain call," critic Dyer of the Boston *Globe* reported, "Ozawa stopped applauding the performers who had joined the audience in applauding him and once more, movingly, pointed upward."

Members of the press—critics, reporters, photographers, magazine writers, and radio and television representatives—have gone along in varying numbers on the orchestra's trips abroad since the first one in 1952. At first eyed with suspicion by some ("It is no pleasure to meet you," Richard Dyer claims a violinist said as they were introduced), these tagalongs are soon accepted into the fold, time and travel being the great levelers that they are. Sometimes they find themselves breaking out of the musical mold—dining at the tradition-steeped Garrick Club in London, or watching *Gone with the Wind* performed as an all-singing, all-dancing extravaganza by the Flower Troupe of the Takarazuka All-Girl Theater, outside Osaka. Principally, however, they are measuring the reactions of foreign audiences to the BSO, and vice versa, and moving along in this world of players from place to place, sharing experiences that can be relayed back home to waiting readers.

In 1971, the Players' Handbook, containing detailed information about the European tour, included a pertinent advisory note:

The writers traveling with us are assigned by their publications and are working just as BSO and staff are. That means, among other things, that all conversations with the press can be considered "on the record," unless specified otherwise. Having a tour reported at home is vitally important to us and assigning these writers to us represents a big investment for their publications; they should be assisted in any way feasible.

In general, the presence of newspersons on BSO tours hasn't proved inhibiting to the business or pleasures of foreign travel. There have, of course, been a few slips of the tongue and subsequently the pen as rapport between musicians and writers increased en route, but more often the growth of a new understanding and respect on both sides has been the consequence.

On the morning after the orchestra's arrival in Japan in 1978, violinist Leonard Moss, who had been there before, led Richard Hammerich of the Springfield *Union* and another journalist on an introductory walk through the hilly, garden-like castle park in Fukuoka. The sun was bright and the air was crisp, and Moss, an avid bird watcher, was carrying his binoculars, but no one was prepared for what they encountered. Thousands of picnicking schoolchildren, none taller than one's heart, seemed to cover every available sandy path and patch of greening grass. Seated in groups of four on blankets or squares of bright plastic, each had an individual lunchbox and Thermos, and although the level of chatter was high-pitched and punctuated with cries and laughter, strenuous horseplay was at a minimum.

Westerners are not uncommon in Fukuoka, but the sight of three visitors in their midst caused a small sensation among the youngsters. The three found themselves besieged on every side by infants bowing from the waist, shaking hands, and shouting, "Hello," "What's your name?," "Goodbye," "Thank you," all in discernible English. One of the trio recalls, "Giggling schoolgirls presented us with items from their lunchboxes—candies, potato chips, and small trinkets, and only the velvet-glove discipline of their teachers prevented them from following us (and our cameras) like the legendary Pied Piper."

When they had extricated themselves, bowing and waving like royalty, the press men thanked their musician guide profusely. "What a welcome, Lenny!" said one; "Lenny, what a story!" said the other.

Travel often inspires musicians to be good cooks or accentuates their appreciation of their own culinary accomplishments. An orchestra trip, particularly abroad, can also bring out the spirit of adventure among the gourmets. The name of the newly discovered, extraordinary, out-of-the-way restaurant, be it in Barcelona or

Kyoto, is guardedly passed along among similarly minded colleagues. Chefs are entreated to divulge exotic recipes, and world-famous eating establishments undergo trials usually reserved for a tyro auditioner. In some cases, the lasting impression of a new city, or even a familiar one, is at least partially taken away on musicians' palates.

A free day on the latest Japanese tour provided a unique experience for orchestra members in the form of a dinner and party at a mountain resort, the Yamanaka Grand Hotel, hosted by music director Seiji Ozawa, impresario Naoyasu Kajimoto, and their wives. From the moment of arrival at this picturesque alpine ryokan, when the Bostonians were met by their hosts and a small army of smiling, bowing inn personnel, the mood was one of relaxation and enjoyment. Rooms were assigned—the nearest to one's preconception of a typical hostelry—and once there, everyone was assisted out of Western clothes and into Japanese dress—a lightweight *yucata* covered with a dark, heavier *dotera*, and wooden clogs replacing shoes. This was the prevailing garb until departure the next morning. Game rooms offered Ping-Pong, pinball machines, and Pachinko (the Japanese pinball craze), among other attractions; several open bars catered to the thirsty; and as a predinner freshener, players slipped into steaming pools (a his and a hers) filled with water from a hot mineral spring. All in all, the evening was a welcome antidote to ten days of intensive work and travel.

Although just about everyone had sat cross-legged in traditional Japanese restaurants before this, the evening's dinner was a new experience. Row upon row of low lacquered tables had a sizable pillow for the diner's back, and a hostess in kimono who served an endless array of delicacies. Meanwhile, on a stage at one end of the banquet hall, Ozawa was presiding over a sake-barrel-breaking ceremony. He was joined by other colleagues for the moment when the lid was finally hammered off and the sake served to one and all in square wooden cups inscribed with the date and site of this special occasion. As the feast proceeded, the stage was occupied by geishas who sang and played native instruments until a white-bearded, fearsomely masked character swept on to do the spectacular Lion Dance. Finally, the geishas led a dance for general participation, a sort of conga line that wove among the less energetic diners. Thereafter, the BSO visitors retired to soft mattresses placed on their bedroom floors, covered themselves with quilts known as *futons*, and slept until a Japanese breakfast was served before departure the next morning.

Except for memories of creature comforts (or discomforts)—understandably important in a one-night-stand schedule—instrumentalists are most apt to remember their tour stops by the auditoriums in which they have played. Although their home base, Symphony Hall, is generally agreed to be one of the acoustical marvels of the world, everyone lends a critical ear to each hall encountered. Arriving for rehearsal, there are those who circle the rim of the stage and clap their hands once or twice while peering into the darkened auditorium. Some scramble up the aisles to the last row of seats to see if conversation onstage can be heard clearly. Others just watch the clappers and the scramblers with a degree of resignation. Here is where the next concert is to be played, come what may.

London's cavernous Royal Albert Hall, where Boston Pops played in 1971 and 1976, was winter-cold for both preconcert rehearsals. Musicians preferred not to shed their heavy weather wear on either occasion, and the piano soloists—Malcolm Frager in layers of sweaters and a scarf, and Ilana Vered wearing coat and gloves—whipped through their concertos with finger preservation foremost in mind.

Arriving at Fukuoka's Shimin Kaikan for the first rehearsal of its 1978 Japanese tour, the orchestra again walked into an unheated hall (fervent apologies and promises by the local management), performed the ritual of acoustical testing, set about a massive tuning ("the flutes are sharp and the clarinets are flat," complained one wind player), temporarily swathed their instruments with jackets and scarves against the March cold, then rehearsed in hats and coats. The ice melted somewhat when Ozawa introduced the Japanese impresario, Mr. Kajimoto, the road manager, Mr. Miyazaki, and the tour staff to the BSO, who reserved its loudest acclaim for Teruo Miyagawa, a Tokyo instrumentalist joining them to play second tuba on the trip. By performance time, the heat was on, and the presence of a capacity audience of 1800 warmed everyone's spirits. It is doubtful, however, if the Shimin Kaikan would make any player's list of the ten best halls.

A poll of players during or after any given concert would not always result in a unanimous opinion, but among the favorites to be mentioned in the next breath after Symphony Hall might be Vienna's mellow Musikvereinsaal, the Berlin Philharmonie, Tokyo's Bunka Kaikan, the fantastically embellished Palau in Barcelona, and Amsterdam's Concertgebouw. Acoustical science being the perennial puzzle that it is, live quality versus dryness and reverberatory ambience versus emptiness remain ongoing sources of argument throughout any tour. Where one sits on the platform, whether one is cramped or has plenty of elbow room, also affects the ear of the performer. Inconclusive as these judgments may be, they add a certain zest on the road, with every new place offering a fresh challenge. Ultimate agreement? There's no place like home.

Before they left Japan for home in March of 1978, the Boston Symphony was joined in its final concert at Tokyo's Bunka Kaikan by the student orchestra of the Toho School, alma mater of Seiji Ozawa. The occasion was the world premiere of a piece, *Deai* ("En-

counters"), commissioned by the BSO from Gunther Schuller, who, with Ozawa, was one of the three conductors, 180 instrumentalists, and eight vocalists participating in the performance. The student players, at first divided into two offstage orchestras, gradually appeared onstage individually or in small groups. As the music progressed, they took seats next to a BSO partner to produce a finale signifying total musical agreement. The impact of the tonal unification of experienced BSO sound with that of the highly disciplined Toho group was not lost on the audience. At the concert's end, musicians joined listeners in a unique Japanese tradition—surprisingly, a collective rendition of "Auld Lang Syne."

Several weeks after the musicians had returned from the tour, there was an echo of this moving experience in the form of a brief, neat, handwritten letter from a Toho instrumentalist, posted on the BSO players' bulletin board: "I really appreciate that you gave us a great chance to play together ... Natsuko Oshima."

V
The Players Offstage

When performances are over on tour, BSO musicians are accustomed to climbing into waiting buses and being conveyed to their hotels or to airports where planes will take them to the next stop. In Boston, however, once the concert is over most musicians hastily change into civilian clothes and head for the stage door of Symphony Hall. Some linger to talk with friends in the Hall's corridors or backstage—subscribers and regular Symphony patrons have, over the years, never hesitated to share their enthusiasms and occasional disappointments with members of the orchestra during intermissions and after the performance. Traditionally, BSO players make themselves available for these town-and-gown interchanges, a custom which has done much to weld a valued and continuing relationship between performer and listener in Boston.

However, all playing and no play could make dull people of these talented men and women—a calamity none of the BSO's current instrumentalists has allowed to happen. The late George E. Judd, manager of the orchestra for twenty years until 1954, told Milton Bass of the Berkshire *Eagle* in Pittsfield, Mass.: "I feel that if anybody is going to be interesting at a concert for two hours, he is not going to be uninteresting for the other twenty-two hours that go to make up the day."

More music awaits most of the players beyond Symphony Hall: at home, in the teaching studio, in some related avocation, or through involvement in the community. Just about everyone has found through experience and preference that music remains a common denominator for what happens outside—from bird-watching (and hearing) to restoring an ancient house to its original classic structure.

The musician discovers early on that an orchestra schedule calls for severe adjustments in family living. Morning rehearsals, three abbreviated Thursday morning concerts, Friday matinees, and performances on Saturday, Tuesday, and Thursday evenings—along with local runouts and week-long tours along the Eastern seaboard —largely prevent the BSO musician from indulging in the local suburban social scene.

One brass player said regretfully:

We've lived here for ten years and we hardly know our neighbors. Saturday nights are the get-together times in our town. But I'm playing, and even though the children have grown up, my wife wouldn't think of going out without me. So she has become an orchestra widow, and she accepts it cheerfully, but when I sit there onstage waiting to blow my two-toots-worth, I know she's probably listening to the live broadcast and wondering if it's worth not living like other people. Not that she complains—we go on the foreign tours together, and not everybody can see as much of the world as we have—but I am unhappy that my profession cuts her out of the kind of everyday life that a friendly, open-hearted lady should have.

A veteran orchestra wife said, "We learned a long time ago that our circle of friends would be members of the orchestra. It took a while to realize how inbred we were—how much our lives were tied up with other players, and how closely our social interests depended on those who, in a sense, we had grown up with."

Whether the musician or any performer in the arts can reasonably expect to have the best of both worlds remains problematic. Predictably, the demands of artists' talents remove them, early in the game, from any ordinary regimen of daily living, so that upon arrival at success in their field, they find its mundane consequences must be realized and, if not wholly accepted, at least tolerated. In his autobiography, *Cadenza*, former BSO music director Erich Leinsdorf stated his feeling quite openly about the performer's mission:

Without being in the least naive, I have felt all my life that it is a special advantage of the theatrical and musical professions not to be subject to the routine of regular hours, days, and weeks throughout the year. I consider it something out of the ordinary to perform on holidays, when office and shop are shut and when people look to us for recreation, solace, and pleasure through great music.

The women in the orchestra have also had to make adjustments in their personal lives. They have been faced with questions that women before them seldom encountered. Is it possible to combine a prestigious orchestral position with a workable marriage? While the individual situation obviously determines the viability of the woman musician's private life, there are certain inescapable factors that are not conducive to an evenly regulated marriage. Says one woman:

The biggest problem is scheduling. The woman adjusts, the man doesn't. When he is a nine-to-five worker, she sleeps late after an evening performance, then goes to rehearsal during the day, and is off again at night to the hall, when the husband returns. For the wife, it s an irregular pattern of days and weeks—with tours, concerts, rehearsals, etc. Socializing is at a minimum, although music as a bond is helpful. If the husband is involved in music, as a performer or administrator, he does have some understanding of the innate problems that must be faced.

Women who are free-lance musicians can accommodate themselves more easily to home life, since engagements are usually of short duration or distributed over a defined period. A busy free-lance violinist, wife of a successful professional man, arranged to transfer her activities to another large city when he was reassigned there. Musicians married to musicians have also been able to make a go of it when separation or temperament were not potentials for conflict. However, one who had been a free-lance player before joining an orchestra observed that her transient female colleagues "were either unhappily married or happily single."

Women who have gained positions in major orchestras are "high achievers," in the words of one of them. Like stars in other media, their "prestige and power" as orchestra members make it difficult for them to meet men of similar status in music or out of it. Thus, there is a resultant "fear of marriage" which is based on likely problems of personal and emotional adjustment. Having worked hard to gain enviable artistic and economic status, most are reluctant to yield it for the traditional role of mother and homemaker. Substantial provision for domestic help and child care would be a large inducement, but most women musicians realize that it would take a truly understanding husband indeed who would submit himself completely to her life-style and commitments without regard for his own interests.

"Most male musicians don't have the kind of domestic problems we do," one woman player remarked. "Their wives are supportive. They take care of the laundry and the children, and contact the plumber when the dishwasher refuses to wash. We all make music together on the platform, but for most of the women players these chores remain to be done unless one has a sympathetic relative, an indulgent friend, or can find paid help."

Many wives of musicians will argue with the assertion that their only role is to keep the home fires burning while their husbands fiddle at Symphony Hall. Some have symphony subscriptions or go to concerts of special interest. Others are performers themselves, teach, or have jobs in unrelated fields. Among BSO wives may be found a practicing lawyer, an opera singer, a college lecturer, and the director of a community nursery school. But for those whose career is at home, usually with children, the vagaries of orchestral schedules and the special needs of their spouses are neither surprising nor oppressive. What's more, the longtime friendships which have developed among members of the orchestra and their families have produced a highly sensitive communications system. "Most of the orchestra news comes from the wives," Harry Dickson points out in his book on the BSO. "They seem to have all the secret information about what is going to happen long before it happens." This is not gossip for gossip's sake, but advance notice of changes in schedule, projected tours, and alterations in programs, which, with luck, may give the family an extra night or so together at home.

As for women players, one of them observes, "Most women should decide about marrying and having children when their places in the orchestra are secure, and all circumstances are right." A provision for maternity leave of at least six months is included in the musicians' Trade Agreement to cover this contingency.

One woman musician said:

I thought I'd see what it would be like to have some maternal responsibilities while I was working, so I took several of my teenage students as boarders during a two-month summer session. It was very illuminating. I had to feed them, pick up after them, and have an answer when they'd ask my opinion about almost everything. Without meaning to, they obstructed my work at every turn, and although I hadn't brought them up, it gave me a good idea of the problems that having a family would present. When music is such an important part of one's life, I think there's something to be said for sublimating the need for a family in work at the orchestra, with teaching, in outside affiliations, and in concern for others. As for the myth that successful musicians must have a high degree of sexual orientation, it just isn't true.

Whatever their personal arrangements, women musicians have long since become part of the BSO. Despite heavy rehearsal, performance, teaching, and tour schedules, they, along with their male colleagues, have proven how it is possible for BSO instrumentalists to have full and happy lives at home. The hours may be different from those of their neighbors, and some obscure musical parlance may occasionally be heard, but by and large, their interests are shared. No man is an island, nor woman either, so unlike their early forebears, BSO musicians have integrated themselves into their communities in and around Boston with little or no effort.

Inevitably, when discussing musicians and their children, there are debates about the tendency of progeny to follow in the footsteps of their parents as performers. Three exceptions—violinists Ronald Knudsen and Raymond Sird, and horn player Charles Yancich—embarked on musical careers without family precedent. However, for most of the players, their immediate families as well as the next generation have close ties with music. Two retired first-desk BSO instrumentalists have sons in other orchestras: Roger Voisin's, a third-generation trumpeter, is in the Syracuse Symphony, and bassist Henry Portnoi's, a timpanist, is in the Minnesota Orchestra. BSO violinst Alfred Schneider's son has recently joined the trumpet section of the Pittsburgh Symphony, while George Zazofsky, for twenty-seven years a member of the BSO, had the satisfaction of returning as concertmaster of the Pops Esplanade Orchestra when son Peter, a 1978 bronze medal winner of the Wieniawski Competition in Poland, performed the Tchaikovsky Violin Concerto at Symphony Hall and by the Charles River.

In many families music is a way of life. "Singing or playing almost anything with almost anybody who also likes to sing and play" is a household rule in contrabassoonist Richard Plaster's house, since his wife plays bassoon, his daughter violin, his sons trumpet and bass, and he himself is also a violist. The children, who began their studies early ("lost time in a musical way is irretrievable"), are used to performing for people, are involved at school, and are "proud of knowing." Musical careers in prospect? "Drifting toward it," he thinks.

Like other of his BSO colleagues, Plaster feels that "a great deal depends on the wife" where children's practice habits are concerned. Because of his schedule, he doesn't see them when they return from school and it becomes Mrs. Plaster's responsibility "to make sure they practice, and don't take off for Jane's or Joey's." He is philosophical about directing children toward professional careers in music. "Some find that competition makes them more avid, others don't have the motivation. It can be a heartbreaking business—there are so many factors beyond one's control. It just happened to work in my case."

First oboist Ralph Gomberg was one of seven children in a musical family, and joined four of them as graduates of Curtis Institute. Now, in his own household, music and the arts are of the first importance and his children have been introduced to instruments: his son to the violin, one daughter to the flute, the other to the piano. Mrs. Gomberg, a former professional ballet dancer, is head of the dance department and dean of performing arts at neighboring Walnut Hill School, and a faculty member of the Boston Ballet School.

In first violinist Burton Fine's family, it has proved to be a case of "like father, like son, like mother, like daughter." Son Marshall first studied the violin but now as a graduate student at the University of Michigan has switched to viola; daughter Elaine, now at Juilliard, chose her mother's instrument, the flute. ("There was a good one around the house," Fine explains.)

Violinist Emanuel Boder, who after twenty years in the Leningrad Philharmonic, emigrated in 1976 to the United States with his wife, Anna Belekh, a concert violinist and teacher. They have a violinist son, Alexander, at the Juilliard School where violist Betty Benthin's daughter Jean, a flutist, is also continuing her family tradition.

A wife and daughter who are cellists, and sons who play French horn and piano, contribute to the musical atmosphere in oboist Wayne Rapier's home. One of the BSO's flying enthusiasts (he is a private pilot, Joseph Hearne a commercial pilot, Paul Fried a glider pilot), Rapier also indulges his special interest as a player of Bach in annual appearances at the Bethlehem, Pennsylvania, Bach Festival, and is active in the formation of a group dedicated to performance of the composer's works in Boston.

Husband and wife instrumental duos exist in many combinations. When their schedules permit, violinist Sheila Fiekowsky concertizes with her pianist husband, André-Michel Schub. Cellist Luis Leguia, who has toured as a soloist on five continents, is married to a flutist active both as a recitalist and teacher, while a colleague, cellist Ronald Feldman, is a member of the Greylock Trio with his wife, harpist Elizabeth Morse, and BSO flutist Paul Fried. The Joseph Pietropaolos are a viola-cello combination, and bassoonist Matthew Ruggiero, violinist Michael Vitale, and trombonist Gordon Hallberg have wives who are active professional violinists. Personnel manager William Moyer, former BSO trombonist and an amateur recorder player, shares with his wife Betsy, a harpsichordist, an interest in baroque music. In the family of violinist Gottfried Wilfinger are his wife, a gifted pianist, and of five musically inclined children, one daughter is studying for a career as a flutist.

After exposing their own children to music, and perhaps introducing them to the rudiments, musician parents generally turn them over to other teachers, and they themselves begin teaching others. Principal timpanist Vic Firth has stated: "I feel obliged to teach. It's my obligation to pass on to young people the knowledge it took me twenty-five years to acquire. It's my job, assuming you like my style, to help develop quality in a student; to sharpen and shape their ability."

The presence in Boston and environs of a plethora of educational institutions with music departments has for many years created a demand for the teaching services of Boston Symphony members. New England Conservatory, Boston Conservatory of Music, Boston University's School of Fine Arts, Harvard and Northeastern Universities, Wellesley and Wheaton Colleges, Massachusetts Institute of Technology, Brandeis University, Lowell State, and smaller private music schools have all availed themselves of the opportunity to have BSO instrumentalists on their faculties, and for this privilege have accepted the intricate scheduling processes that must be devised to integrate BSO commitments with institutional teaching time.

While for some younger members teaching is a new experience, there are those in the BSO for whom it has become a major interest in life. Cellist Mischa Nieland, with the orchestra since 1943, husband of an accomplished musician and medical editor, and father of a physician violinist, acquired an interest in teaching early in his career while studying at Peabody Conservatory, Baltimore, with the renowned pedagogue Diran Alexanian. Violinist Gerald Gelbloom, who joined the violin section in 1961, admits to devoting himself to "all the music I can do and hear and teach," an ambition filled by a full schedule of performance and students. The late flutist James Pappoutsakis, who retired after forty-one years in the BSO, continued to teach. He believed that:

One's success with an instrument is formed by one's own personality plus the genealogy of study with one special teacher. The student represents the teacher's thinking, if it's good, and the teacher should be the only authority while studying—after that they're on their own. This way everyone becomes a distinct artist with a recognizable sound. It's not wise to work with too many teachers—the result can only be a nonindividualistic style. Some other pitfalls for young players? Thinking that to play at one's most beautiful is best, and that the conductor will decide how much more or less is required, or that interpreting on a decibel basis will represent the composer's state of mind. What everyone should realize is that any performance should reflect every nuance one is capable of; subtleties are noticeable—if it doesn't come easily, something is wrong.

Understandably, musicians of BSO caliber have plenty to say to promising instrumentalists. At Boston University's School of Music alone, there are thirty-four present or former members from the orchestra on the faculty, while New England and Boston Conservatories and the universities and colleges in and around Boston have their complement. Principal oboist Ralph Gomberg finds teaching "a response to the idealism that creates musicians. It's part of a self-fulfilling prophecy that one's convictions and their accomplishment will go on."

A new aspect of the players' mission was introduced in 1978, when at the close of the Berkshire Festival at Tanglewood, BSO musicians pledged to found an annual fellowship at the Berkshire Music Center, honoring retiring manager Tod Perry, to benefit a minority instrumentalist. This concern of many orchestra personnel has also taken the form of a suggestion to the BSO Overseers' Personnel Relations Committee, which has players' representation, that a program be developed by the orchestra through which BSO members would be available on a volunteer basis to teach underprivileged minority students in the Greater Boston area. As a community-related project, it could provide talented individuals with an expert source of instruction which the public school system is economically unable to provide. Here also would be an opportunity to widen the musical horizons of young instrumentalists beyond the point of playing popular music exclusively.

Beyond local teaching, orchestra members take time to become involved with young musicians and listeners. An ongoing program between the BSO and Holy Trinity, an Episcopalian school in Haiti with a music department and orchestra, invites BSO musicians to visit and assist briefly in the development of a struggling but no less determined enterprise conceived to open up youthful native performing instincts. English horn player Laurence Thorstenberg and violinist Max Hobart are among the most recent visitors to Port-au-Prince in this program. There is also enthusiastic support among the musicians for the Foster Parents Plan, of which Marylou Speaker is the BSO correspondent. Through the plan, the orchestra has adopted three children—one each in Bolivia, Ecuador, and Bali.

Closer to home, Youth Concerts at Symphony Hall, conducted by Harry Ellis Dickson and administered by Anita Kurland, have become a tradition over two decades. Although a few childrens' concerts had been given in the orchestra's earliest years, and Boston was one of seventeen American and European cities to engage Ernest Schelling and his New York Philharmonic Children's Concerts format in 1924, the BSO's attempts to build a future audience had been sporadic. In 1959, Dickson, with the aid of a "dedicated committee," revived the concept of a concert series specifically for youngsters with members of the Boston Symphony comprising the majority of the orchestra. The series now consists of four series of three morning programs each, gauged to the interests and attention span of students in grades five to ten.

Today, mixed media and aspects of participation both by the youthful audiences and aspiring performers have contributed markedly to the success of the concept, thus furthering Schelling's then-innovative use of lantern slides, song sheets, and student notebook competitions. According to Howard Shanet in his orchestral biography, *Philharmonic*, Schelling used his collection of 5000 slides, hand-colored on glass and valued at over $25,000—"pictures of musical instruments of all ages and countries, of composers and how they lived, and of every other subject that lent itself to visual illustration in connection with his programs."

Nowadays, films, projections of artwork produced by members of the youth audience, and solo appearances by their talented contemporaries continue to enliven these introductory concerts. Annually, a competition coordinated with the music departments of Boston-area schools results in the choice of at least five from as many as fifty applicants to be soloists in the season's concerts. Thus, the immediacy of music is brought home to the eyes and ears of the listeners by performers in their own age brackets. Already two competitors in these contests have gone on to become Boston Symphony members—violinist Ronan Lefkowitz and bassist Lawrence Wolfe.

Harry Dickson, like Arthur Fiedler before him, is among numerous BSO musicians who have always been interested in conducting. Fiedler, a string and keyboard player in the orchestra, left in 1930 to devote full time to Boston Pops. The BSO's two most recent concertmasters, Richard Burgin and Joseph Silverstein, besides being its assistant conductors, have conducted outside Symphony Hall. Burgin, since his retirement, has become music director of a Florida orchestra, and Silverstein has led symphonic organizations in Los Angeles, Rochester, and Jerusalem, as well as presiding over his student Boston University Orchestra in its prizewinning participation in the 1976 Herbert von Karajan competition for youth orchestras in Berlin. E. Fernandez Arbos, once a BSO principal violinist, returned as a guest conductor in 1931, while Nikolai

Sokoloff, a onetime BSO player, departed later to become music director of the Cleveland Orchestra.

As might be expected, the orchestra still contains a number of musicians who take to the podiums of outside organizations whenever their schedules permit. While not to be construed as rebellion against conductors under whom they have played, the desire to conduct "one's own orchestra" has remained a strong one in many instrumentalists. What impels players to take up the baton? There are as many answers as there are embryo conductors, but a BSO musician without such ambitions feels there are two disparate impulses that drive two different types of musicians to center stage: a powerful desire to control surrounding sound, born perhaps of a resolution to be second fiddle to no one; and an obsessive ear in performance for the twelve lines of the orchestral score (a not uncommon phenomenon among ensemble players) which only a conductor can realize in proper proportion.

Of all BSO personnel, the conducting record is clearly held by violinist Rolland Tapley, who retired from the orchestra in 1978 after fifty-eight years of service. His interest in developing appreciation of symphonic music in outlying communities resulted in his heading the North Shore Philharmonic (north of Boston) for twenty-five seasons, the Wellesley, Massachusetts, Symphony for twenty-four, and the New Hampshire Philharmonic for fourteen. Many of his BSO colleagues joined him in principal-desk positions and as soloists. When he stepped down from the North Shore position, he passed it on to his younger violin partner, Max Hobart, who shared his interest in conducting. Hobart studied at the University of Southern California, and played in the orchestras of New Orleans, Washington, and Cleveland before joining the BSO in 1965. He teaches at New England Conservatory and at Boston University, where the opportunity to work with student orchestras has increased the conducting skills which he uses as director of the North

Shore Philharmonic and other community groups. At North Shore he conducts from sixty-five to seventy volunteer musicians of all ages, to whom he communicates the techniques "stored up" from observing BSO conductors. In addition to being assistant concertmaster of Boston Pops, Hobart has devised and promoted a highly prized item—the Arthur Fiedler wristwatch.

Other communities near Boston have formed orchestras of their own with local musicians, thanks to the initiative of BSO players-turned-conductors. Alfred Schneider, who came to Boston in 1955, founded the Framingham Symphony and conducted it for seven years, later returning as soloist. Egyptian-born, French-trained violinist Michel Sasson annually directs two orchestras in outlying Boston communities, namely the Newton and Brockton Symphonies, both of which he founded. In Brockton, he has featured one fully staged opera each season employing area singers, while in Newton, premieres of unusual music, both classic and modern, have contributed substantially to the growth of community interest in a locally based enterprise. Sasson also finds time to be music director of the Boston Ballet, and has guest conducted the American Ballet Theater in New York and the Boston Pops in Symphony Hall. He was the organizer of a chamber orchestra which gave free concerts of works by Bach and Mozart on the Esplanade under city auspices, and otherwise has put to good use his Paris conducting lessons with Fourestier and Bigot.

Chamber music, at home or in a community recital setting, is an offstage preoccupation of most orchestral players. At Tanglewood, for instance, Max Hobart and his students are often joined in off-hours chamber music sessions by comedian Sam Levenson, a Berkshire resident and astute violinist. Besides many casual or pickup groups, meeting the way others indulge in an evening of bridge, there are numerous active concert-giving music ensembles ranging in repertory from classics to the latest in contemporary confections.

Acorn Street on Boston's Beacon Hill is the setting for the orchestra's jazz-loving ensemble, WUZ. From left are bass Leslie Martin, percussionists Arthur Press and Thomas Gauger, and clarinetist Felix Viscuglia.

Seizing time provided by a BSO rehearsal break, the Incredible String Quartet, a pop music foursome—from left, Robert Olson, John Salkowski, Joseph Hearne, and Lawrence Wolfe—practice in a Symphony Hall corridor.

Challenging all comers at home and on tour, the BSO Softball Team braves hand and facial injuries in the name of active sport. Included are BSO players Rolf Smedvig, Ronald Barron, Richard Mackey, David Ohanian, Ronald Feldman, Paul Fried, Lawrence Wolfe, and Ronald Wilkison.

An interest in exploring the extensive and little-known literature for brass instruments led to the formation of the Empire Brass Quintet, now comprised of three young BSO players—Rolf Smedvig, trumpet; David Ohanian, French horn; and Norman Bolter, trombone—with two others from outside the orchestra. Not only has the quintet distinguished itself as winner of the Naumburg Foundation ensemble competition, made several European and United States tours, and recorded seldom-heard music for combinations of brass instruments, but it has been chosen to play for such state occasions as the Bicentennial visit of Queen Elizabeth of England, and the inauguration of President Jimmy Carter.

Collage, an ensemble specializing in contemporary music, was conceived by percussionist Frank Epstein in the aftermath of a faculty recital of modern works at New England Conservatory. Joining him were violinist Ronald Knudsen, cellist Ronald Feldman, and flutist Paul Fried from the orchestra, with three others—soprano, clarinet, and piano. Touring when schedules permit, Collage presents an annual series of concerts at Boston's Museum of Fine Arts, has made first-time recordings of a number of contemporary works and, in addition to playing a sizable list of world and U.S. premieres, has commissioned music from prominent forward-looking composers.

The WUZ, dedicated to the performance of jazz in a concert context, is a unique combination of BSO players—Leslie Martin, bass; Felix Viscuglia, clarinet; and Arthur Press and Thomas Gauger, percussion. All of these musicians having grown up as performers of popular music, albeit with their sights set on symphony positions, they have welcomed the opportunity to return to their preclassical roots as a contrast to BSO repertory. Although symphony members are always received with deference in Boston, the WUZ have not always been accorded such special treatment. Once, handsomely attired for for a publicity photograph, they brought their jazz instruments to a venerable byway on Boston's Beacon Hill only to be chased away by an indignant Brahmin lady whose front door appeared in the background.

A repertory of a different kind is explored by the New England Harp Trio, formed by harpist Ann Hobson, with BSO colleagues Lois Schaefer, flute, and Carol Procter, cello. Speaking for the group, Miss Procter, who joined the BSO in 1965, says:

> When one joins as a young player, the BSO is first regarded as a stepping-stone to a solo career, but then comes the choice between freedom and security. As one "grows up" the incredible security becomes apparent, and it's easy to become spoiled and complacent—the orchestra schedule drains, and it's hard to find rehearsal time for personal growth. But time can be found if you really mean business. That's why quartets and groups of all kinds are formed—to make headway artistically. Our trio is one of those, put together so that our own musical ideas won't be wasted or lost in an atmosphere where someone is telling you what to do all the time. It's good for keeping up our technique individually, and bringing to our performances with the orchestra something more than comes out of everyday rehearsals. It's good to have lots of room to grow.

Four players of the deep-voiced double bass have also found a way of lightening their somber orchestral tasks by forming the Incredible String Quartet. Joseph Hearne, Robert Olson, John Salkowski, and Lawrence Wolfe, aware of the seldom-exploited potential of their instrument, banded together to make arrangements of popular tunes of the past and present and play them with a haunting understatement that invariably astonishes and delights the unsuspecting. At a Foreign Correspondents Club luncheon honoring Seiji Ozawa during the BSO's 1978 tour of Japan, they provided an enthusiastically greeted prelude to Ozawa's meeting with the international press in Tokyo and demonstrated the many-sided accomplishments of Western musicians and of those in the "fantastic" BSO in particular.

When they were faculty members at Boston Conservatory, violinists Alfred Schneider and Raymond Sird, violist Earl Hedberg, and former BSO cellist Karl Zeise, founded the Gabrielli String Quartet, which has continued to concertize in the metropolitan Boston area, while Bernard Kadinoff, who came to the orchestra in 1951 from the NBC Symphony and is on the music faculty of Boston University, performs as a solo violist and as a member of the Boston Fine Arts Ensemble. Cellist Joel Moerschel teaches at both Wellesley and Wheaton Colleges, and plays with the Wheaton Trio. Membership in the Milwaukee String Quartet when he was assistant concertmaster of that city's symphony has led Bo Youp Hwang to continue his interest in chamber music with the Cremona String Quartet in Boston.

The "reaffirmation of one's solo potential," as violinist Marylou Speaker puts it, persists in string players. "It's a challenge we can't ignore," she says, "even though joining an orchestra means coming to grips with not being a soloist above all." Whenever a heavy schedule permits it, she and other BSO members revert to this different kind of performing. Both she and colleague Cecylia Arzewski have participated in the Wieniawski International Competition in Poland, and have appeared in solo recitals in Boston and New York. Violinist Amnon Levy, who was a soloist with Israeli orchestras before joining the BSO in 1964, has since made solo appearances with both Boston Pops and the Esplanade Orchestra, as have many other BSO instrumentalists.

Players, their wives, and friends who are interested in performing baroque music on ancient instruments are recruited annually during the Tanglewood season for concerts by the Curtisville Consortium, founded by personnel manager Bill Moyer and his wife Betsy. Performances are given in Citizens Hall in a small hamlet down the lake from the Berkshire Festival grounds, with a semistaged production as the finale of the summer's activities. Music by Purcell for *The Tempest* and *The Fairy Queen,* and an Elizabethan wedding masque have been presented in past years enlisting the volunteer services of members of the BSO community for rare opportunities to play baroque flute and violin, viola d'amore, gamba, vertical viola, natural horn, recorder, and virginal, as well as modern instruments. Proceeds from these intimate presentations go toward the restoration of Citizens Hall.

Individual musical accomplishments as well as hidden talents and avocations come to light during the annual four-day BSO fund-raising "Musical Marathon." During this time, tapes of past BSO performances are broadcast and orchestra members offer inducements to the public via radio and television in return for specified contributions.

Many have found that the way to contributors' hearts is frequently gustatory: a special oatmeal bread "made from a secret recipe" by violinist Leonard Moss; a "mystery dessert for eight" concocted by principal flutist Doriot Anthony Dwyer; or a chocolate rum cake ("plenty of rum"), the invention of Ronan Lefkowitz, violinist. Complete dinners for from one to four couples are also among the premiums. "Many splendored" Chinese dishes, prepared by the David Ohanians, and authentic Hungarian fare served by Mr. and Mrs. Bela Wurtzler have proved to be popular, as have "wine and beer, cheese and cheer," offered by percussionist Arthur Press and his wife at their Tanglewood retreat after a festival concert. Appetites are guaranteed for a Berkshire picnic following a bicycle ride with Gordon Hallberg, trombonist and champion cyclist, and in Boston dinner is shared after a session at the ice-skating rink with bassist John Barwicki, an indoor-outdoor sports enthusiast.

Cellist Luis Leguia and violinist Sheldon Rotenberg have proven to be formidable singles tennis opponents for Marathon donors. The BSO Softball Team, captained by trombonist Ron Barron, has had impressive wins on three continents, and boasts among its regulars such string, wind, and brass players as Ed Barker, Ron Feldman, Paul Fried, Dick Mackey, David Ohanian, Rolf Smedvig, and Ron Wilkison. It challenges all comers in Boston or at Tanglewood.

Lovers of unusual forms of locomotion have shared their enthusiasm with bassist-pilot Joseph Hearne on a glider trip, with former executive director Thomas Perry at the wheel of his 1935 Ford convertible for a Berkshire joyride, with principal bassoonist Sherman Walt on his motorcycle for a whirlwind tour of country roads, and aboard ship with John Salkowski, bassist and lobster-fisherman, for a trip around Boston Harbor.

More often than not, music suggests the subjects for principal trumpet Armando Ghitalla's cartoons, the drawings and paintings of violinist Harvey Seigel, and Jerome Rosen's satiric poems. Percussionist Charles Smith has devised a serious live presentation called *Percussion as Therapy* for schools and organizational groups, and a not-so-profound percussion recording of *Background Music for Family Arguments*. Emanuel Borok, who became assistant concertmaster of the BSO in 1974, relates his history of training and experiences in Russia before emigrating to the United States in "The Saga of a Soviet Union Violinist," a pertinent face-to-face talk by a thoughtful and engaging recent arrival.

Recitals, lessons, and group appearances by BSO musicians are also available to Marathon contributors. As many as fifty may hear a demonstration on the Symphony Hall organ by Berj Zamkochian, the BSO's official organist, and opportunities are offered to tyro conductors to lead the Boston Pops or the North Shore Philharmonic in a single number. A violin recital by Marylou Speaker "in your home or mine" has brought as many as sixty listeners to her home, a suburban Boston Victorian house with a high-ceilinged room and small balcony, ideal for chamber music. A baroque concert version (in costume) of Shakespeare's *The Tempest*, with

148 COMMUNITY OF SOUND

Henry Purcell's score, and narration by WGBH announcer William Pierce, is the contribution of the Old Curtisville Players and Singers, organized by William and Betsy Moyer, with BSO musicians playing period instruments. The Marathon list is infinite and revealing—and no matter how seemingly unrelated, music is never far away.

For some, interests range beyond music and the "Musical Marathon" and follow more unusual paths. Violinist Laszlo Nagy, who joined the BSO in 1944, has long been associated with the Jimmy Fund, a Boston-based clinic which has pioneered in the development of chemotherapy treatment for cancer in children. Medical research also continues to be an off-time involvement. Retired violist George Humphrey, in addition to a second career as a maker of stringed instruments, was a member of a mathematical research group at the Massachusetts Institute of Technology studying the effect of music on the brain. Similarly, the late violist Reuben Green devised a program of music therapy which could be taught at the university or medical-school level.

Restoration of venerable houses in the Boston area and near Tanglewood continues to occupy violist Robert Barnes and trumpeter Armando Ghitalla, while woodworking—from building furniture to barns—is a pastime for trumpeter Andre Come, bassist Joe Hearne, and clarinetist Peter Hadcock. Among cellists, Jerome Patterson is a serious chess player, while Jonathan Miller is a postconcert astronomer. A genealogical study of his family and forebears dating back to 1750 occupies contrabassoonist Richard Plaster's spare time, while in a musical context, French horn player Richard Mackey, who came to the BSO in 1973 after engagements with orchestras in Detroit, Cleveland, New Orleans, and Japan, seeks out all available Koechel-listed recordings of Mozart's works —his collection being called by the curator of the British Institute of Recorded Sound "the largest and greatest" in the world. While records are still being assembled, it is Mackey's ambition to tape all of his Mozart recordings consecutively from Opus 1 on. Trombonist Gordon Hallberg, impressed by the breath control techniques of professional vocalists, has found that singing lessons not only aid his brass playing but have revealed a bass voice worthy of cultivation.

Summers spent in Vermont at the Marlboro Festival gave principal clarinetist Harold Wright and his flutist wife a taste for the New England countryside. They built a farm home there, and during the sixteen seasons he participated in the festival, the Wrights and their two sons became enamored of country living. When he joined the BSO in 1970 after a number of years in the National Symphony in Washington, where he had met his wife, the farm was nearer, both to Boston and Tanglewood, and has become a part-week summer residence and skiing destination on free winter weekends. "I'm interested in everything about food," Wright says, "growing it, harvesting it, processing it, cooking it, and eating it. And it's all right there, for part of the year at least."

When Lois Schaefer takes a vacation from the piccolo, she may head for one of her large gardens of flowers and vegetables, either at home outside Boston or near her summer place at Tanglewood. She also may go fishing and camping in her native Northwest. Another gardener, cellist Martha Babcock, is a member of the Massachusetts Horticultural Society, while Ralph Pottle, French horn player in the BSO since 1966, has a specialized gardening hobby—"raising and eating herbs"—and finds kindred souls in the Boston Mycological Club.

The past and future are interests of some BSO players: violist Earl Hedberg collects Americana, from Indian artifacts to iron still banks; trombonist Norman Bolter is intrigued by UFOs, psychic phenomena, and "far-out things," and admits to "enjoying music even when I'm not playing, and watching people who love it, and feeling sorry for those who don't." A different kind of involvement for many players outside Symphony Hall is "Days in the Arts at Tanglewood," a seven-week program begun by the orchestra in 1970 with the cooperation of Massachusetts educational and arts agencies, and of private foundations and sponsors. As many as fifty schoolchildren of differing backgrounds are brought each week from urban and suburban Boston to spend five days at Tanglewood, where they are not only shown the workings of the Boston Symphony, but introduced to professional dance workshops, theaters, and art museums in the Berkshire area. Musicians offer closeup views of their instruments—the visitors are even given a chance to try some of them—and sports and games are planned to dispel any idea of pedantry. For many youngsters, "Days in the Arts" is an introduction not only to the arts, but to the countryside—and an opportunity for musicians to reexamine and explain their calling in the most basic terms.

In Boston's schools, also, demonstrations of instruments by their BSO exponents have proved fascinating to middle-grade students and their teachers alike. Among them, Ralph Pottle's saga of the evolution of the French horn ("a plumber's nightmare") from the Australian conch shell ("an accident of nature discovered when human power was applied") to other members of the brass family —from hollowed-out logs and cows' horns to the sophisticated instruments of today—are amusing and revelatory. How the hunting horn was written into early opera, and why brass assumed a stately, ceremonial role in music are engagingly explored in Pottle's analysis.

Although without pretensions to becoming captains of industry, there are BSO members whose chosen instruments have created interesting sidelines for them. From the standpoint of variety and inventiveness, the percussion section is an enclave in itself. Principal timpanist Vic Firth, a big-game hunter, an automotive buff, and a collector of American art, also handles a custom line of percussion accessories. "As a student, I could never find a stick that satisfied me, so I decided to make my own. I discovered that maple was more resilient than hickory—now all of them are maple and hand turned. Since I won't market inferior sticks, we use the rejects for kindling!"

Thomas Gauger also has a small business for the manufacturer of drumsticks, but most of his spare time is spent either with the BSO jazz-oriented WUZ quartet, or participating in outside sports with his large family. Before joining the BSO in 1963, he had been a member of the ensemble formed by musical innovator Harry Partch.

Also a sports enthusiast and performer with the WUZ, Arthur Press founded a workshop for aspiring percussionists, and in addition to extensive teaching joins his wife in overseeing the musical education of their children, a pianist and a violinist. "We feel that encouragement is the key to progress on a chosen instrument—compliments when they're deserved go farther than pointing out faults," he says. A graduate of the Juilliard School after growing up in both popular and classic surroundings, Press played in the Radio City Music Hall orchestra and in the Little Orchestra of New York before joining the BSO in 1956.

Wooden handles for "symphonic castanets," invented and manufactured by Frank Epstein, are now used by most major orchestras throughout the world. The castanets, required for numerous symphonic repertory pieces, approximate the sound produced by individual players. "To dancers," he explains, "castanets are like life. They reveal individual personalities by passing on through sound the impulses each hand expresses. Dancers choose them like instruments—all sizes, high and low in radiation, masculine and feminine." Epstein imports castanets from Spain, after which wooden handles (more responsive than plastic) are affixed. When used in an orchestral context, these castanets permit the percussionist to reflect gradations in tone and expression with great subtlety.

Dutch-born Epstein, whose early training was as a pianist, changed to percussion in junior high school in California. He went on to study with William Kraft and received his degree from the University of Southern California. Slated for a third summer as a Fellow at the Berkshire Music Center, he instead joined the BSO in May 1968. Several years later, he organized the contemporary music group, Collage. Epstein represents the BSO in purchase of unusual percussion instruments required for Indian, Latin, African, or Japanese works, as well as those which appear unexpectedly in the more avant-garde repertory.

Although he claims to have become a percussionist in order to break an apartment lease, Charles Smith, who joined the orchestra in 1943, came from a family with two generations of musical credentials. After attending Juilliard, he played six-hundred performances of Gershwin's *Porgy and Bess* on tour, and has since become the center of a household which includes his violinist wife Josephine, and three accomplished daughters, one of whom, Joanne, has made three solo piano appearances with the Esplanade Orchestra. A gourmet Italian cook, a collector of percussion cartoons, and an honorary member of Pi Kappa Lauda, he has yet to miss a BSO rehearsal or performance commitment in thirty-five years.

The community that is the Boston Symphony comes into being in a very special way. Unlike a neighborhood or social club, it is not populated as the result of the urging of friends. As tightly knit as the musicians' world may be, the newest arrival may still be one whose antecedents are mostly unfamiliar. But because the orchestra membership now plays an important part in the choice of colleagues, the newcomer is already assured of understanding and acceptance on the acknowledged common denominator—musical excellence. It is virtually impossible to be a loner in a symphony orchestra since the basic reason for any one person to be there is the same reason for everyone.

How one lives outside the framework of the Symphony Hall schedule is, nevertheless, a private affair. Cliques based on common interests inevitably form, and among orchestra colleagues, the nonmusical talents or hobbies are soon discovered by kindred souls. One learns quickly whose social, political, and moral views are congenial, but since the shared effort is musicmaking, these issues are largely relegated to discussion outside Symphony Hall.

Freedom, satisfaction, and happiness in their private lives were called contributing factors to musicians' "perfection in their work" by music director Emil Paur in 1893, a judgment the convolutions of time and custom have not altered substantially. Unquestionably what retired manager Tod Perry described as "the provincial setting" in which the BSO is "the fountainhead of musical activity" and a recognized social institution, has furthered the desirability of living and working in Boston. For its dedicated players the world of the BSO has proved to be the best imaginable in which to find themselves.

Afterword

Aaron Copland, in his foreword to Constantine Manos's *Portrait of a Symphony*, observes: "Everyone from the ticket-taker to the man who encases the harp for the night is charged with the glamour of an orchestra."

Audiences from the top balcony to the first row on the main floor, managers and secretaries, house staff and backstage crew, time after time, are drawn into the miraculous spell this world of players can evoke. Manos comments on the audience:

Some Bostonians have owned the same seats in Symphony Hall for fifty years. They are often the first to arrive for a concert, sitting quietly in the dim stillness waiting for the Hall to come to life around them. Many of them first came to "Symphony" as children and still remember the wonder of that experience. Time is the difference between fascination and devotion. This is the process which has brought the Orchestra a devoted following and made Symphony Hall a temple and a landmark.

As concertmaster Joseph Silverstein has pointed out, with orchestra, staff, management, and trustees all under one roof, "it is almost impossible not to know who everyone is." Familiarity is somehow conveyed to first visitors to Symphony Hall as well as to listeners who experience the Boston Symphony away from home. Good feeling and proximity among the musicians and those with whom they work, an ambience now so traditional that it scarcely needs nurturing, accounts for much of the appeal that the BSO radiates internationally and at Symphony Hall. A house handyman, perhaps not readily identifiable as the Beethoven buff he happens to be, is particularly happy when his job takes him within listening distance of the auditorium during rehearsal time. "I polish the brass, and they pay me for it!" he confides with some wonder.

The players, collectively and individually the objects of admiration and curiosity, continue to have their exits and their entrances, and to play many parts. The BSO cycle, as it reaches its hundredth year, seems destined to fulfill founder Henry Higginson's hope, expressed in 1888: ". . . if it can be made to continue forever, which is my expectation, so much the better."

Notes

Chapter 1

1. Unless otherwise indicated in text, all quotes in this chapter are from *The Boston Symphony Orchestra, 1881–1931* by M. A. DeWolfe Howe. This includes the quote by Louis C. Elson, the quote from *Music*, and the quote from the Boston *Advertiser*.
2. *It's All in the Music: The Life and Work of Pierre Monteux* by Doris Monteux, p. 109.
3. Monteux, p. 113.
4. *Symphony Hall, Boston* by H. Earle Johnson, p. 95.
5. Monteux, p. 115.

Chapter 3

1. Unless otherwise indicated in text, all quotes in this chapter are from *The Boston Symphony Orchestra, 1881–1931* by M. A. DeWolfe Howe.
2. *Symphony Hall, Boston* by H. Earle Johnson, p. 59.
3. Johnson, p. 69.
4. From "Koussevitzky in 1974, A Centennial Tribute" by Paul Fromm, reproduced in BSO program of October 10, 11, 12, and 22, 1974.
5. From BSO program of August 19, 1972.
6. From review by Louis Snyder in the *Christian Science Monitor*, July 2, 1971.
7. From review by Louis Snyder in the *Christian Science Monitor*, July 31, 1974.
8. Johnson, p. 23.

Chapter 4

1. Unsigned interview in *The Musician*, June 1908, Volume 6, p. 13.
2. Pan Pacific BSO program clips (May 14–27, 1915), Boston Public Library, Brown Collection.
3. Ibid.
4. Japanese reviews from Press Office, Symphony Hall, Boston.

Bibliography

The author and the photographer are indebted to each member of the Boston Symphony for contributing to this book, through conversations, observations, and often merely by being visible when the camera clicked. Equally appreciated is the cooperation of management, of the Symphony Hall staff, and of those outside constituents to whom the orchestra has become an integral part of life.

Know Your Orchestra, the biographical handbook published annually by the Council of the BSO, has been an invaluable source of information. Thanks also to Harry Ellis Dickson, Leslie Martin, and Matthew Ruggiero for material written specifically for this book, and to Louis Speyer for excerpts from a personal memoir. Personnel managers William Moyer and Harry Shapiro, their assistant Patricia Boscio, members of the press department, and Thomas D. Perry, Jr., are among many who have cheerfully supplied answers to obscure questions large and small. To Beacon Press editors Luna Carne-Ross, who helped shape the concept of this book, and Joanne Wyckoff, who has brought it into print, we are understandably grateful.

Books

Dickson, Harry Ellis. *"Gentlemen, More Dolce Please!"* Boston: Beacon Press, 1969.

Howe, M. A. DeWolfe, revised and extended in collaboration with John N. Burk. *The Boston Symphony Orchestra, 1881–1931.* Boston: Houghton Mifflin, 1931.
Humphrey, Martha Burnham. *An Eye for Music.* Boston: H. M. Teich, 1949.
Johnson, H. Earle. *Symphony Hall, Boston.* Boston: Little Brown, 1950.
King's Handbook of Boston. Boston: Moses King Corporation, 1889.
Kupferberg, Herbert. *Tanglewood.* New York: McGraw Hill, 1976.
Leinsdorf, Erich. *Cadenza, A Musical Career.* Boston: Houghton Mifflin, 1976.
Manos, Constantine. *Portrait of a Symphony.* New York: Basic Books, 1960.
Monteux, Doris. *It's All in the Music: The Life and Work of Pierre Monteux.* New York: Farrar, Straus and Giroux, 1965.
Munch, Charles. *I Am a Conductor.* New York: Oxford University Press, 1955.
Seltzer, George. *The Professional Symphony Orchestra.* Metuchen, N.J.: Scarecrow Press, 1975.
Shanet, Howard. *Philharmonic—A History of New York's Orchestra.* New York: Doubleday, 1975.
Smith, Moses. *Koussevitzky.* New York: Allen, Towne and Heath, 1947.
Swoboda, Henry, ed. *The American Symphony Orchestra.* New York: Basic Books, 1967.
Thomas, Theodore, edited by George P. Upton. *A Musical Autobiography.* Chicago: A. C. McClerg, 1905.
Woodworth, G. Wallace. *The World of Music.* Boston: Harvard University Press, 1946.

Articles

Bass, Milton, *Berkshire Eagle,* August 7, 1952.
Detroit *News,* May 17, 1977, unsigned interview with Doriot Dwyer.
Durgin, Cyrus, European trip reports reprinted by Boston *Globe,* 1952.
Dyer, Richard, European trip reports reprinted from Boston *Globe,* 1976.
Dyer, Richard, Boston *Globe,* October 1, 1976.
Eckert, Thor, *Christian Science Monitor,* April 5, 1978.
Miller, Margo, Boston *Globe,* March 13, 1977.
Pan Pacific BSO program clips (May 14–27, 1915), Boston Public Library, Brown Collection.
Pfeifer, Ellen, Boston *Herald American,* September 3, 1978.

Pincus, Andrew L., *Berkshire Eagle,* July 17, 1978.
Schwarzbaum, Lisa, *Real Paper,* April 23, 1975.
Snyder, Louis, *Christian Science Monitor,* April 16–May 4, 1971, July 2, 1971, and July 31, 1974.
Storer, H. J., "The Story of the Founding of the Boston Symphony Orchestra," *The Musician,* November 1908.
Suarez, Therese, *France Amerique,* October 30, 1975.
Taylor, Nora, *Christian Science Monitor,* October 14, 1977.
Walter, W. E., "Touring With an Orchestra," *Harper's Weekly,* March 29, 1913.

Index

Alexanian, Diran, 137
Alpert, Victor, 64–65, 85
Arbos, E. Fernandez, 140
Arzewski, Cecylia, 145

Babcock, Martha, 149
Bailey, Lillian, 8
Bailly, Louis, 37
Banks, Talcott M., 121
Barker, Edwin, 51–52, 147
Barnes, Robert, 148
Barron, Ronald, 57, 146
Barwicki, John, 87–88, 92, 146
Bass, Milton, 129
Bedetti, Jean, 33
Beecham, Sir Thomas, 40
Belekh, Anna, 136
Beneke, Tex, 37
Benthin, Betty, 77, 136
Benthin, Jean, 136
Bernstein, Leonard, 36
Boder, Alexander, 136
Boder, Emanuel, 136
Bolter, Norman, 35–36, 143, 149–150
Borok, Emanuel, 15, 147
Brennan, William H., 96–97
Burgin, Richard, 17, 46, 50, 53, 63, 140

Cabot, Frederick P., 16, 18
Cabot, Henry B., 49, 81, 90
Cage, John, 74
Came, Louise, 39, 116

Cardillo, Pasquale, 28–29
Casals, Pablo, 55
Casella, Alfredo, 80
Child, Julia, 47
Chobanian, Dr. Keran, 115–116
Come, Andre, 148
Copland, Aaron, 154
Crumb, George, 74–75

Dane, Ernest B., 18–19
Davis, Colin, 45
Del Negro, Ferdinand, 55
Del Tredici, David, 75
Dickson, Harry Ellis, 63, 67, 89, 133, 139, 140
Downes, Olin, 72, 96
Durgin, Cyrus, 108, 114
Dwyer, Doriot Anthony, 33, 52–53, 146
Dyer, Richard, 74, 110–111, 118, 122–123

Elias, Gerald, 25
Ellis, Charles A., 95–96, 97
Elson, Louis C., 9
Epstein, Frank, 78, 143, 151–152
Eskin, Jules, 50–51

Fahnestock, Mrs. Harris, 121
Farrar, Geraldine, 96
Feder, Donn-Alexandre, 89
Feldman, Ronald, 33, 136, 143, 147

162 INDEX

Fiedler, Arthur, 65, 79–80, 87, 89, 90, 110, 140, 142
Fiedler, Emanuel, 12, 77
Fiedler, Max, 12, 71
Fiekowsky, Sheila, 33–34, 136
Fine, Burton, 50–51, 56, 70–71, 77, 135–136
Fine, Elaine, 136
Fine, Marshall, 135–136
Firth, Everett, 57–58, 120, 137, 150–151
Fourel, Georges, 36
Fradkin, Fredric, 16
Frager, Malcolm, 126
Fried, Paul, 136, 143, 147
Fromm, Paul, 73

Galamian, Ivan, 50
Garber, Jan, 40
Gardiner, Mrs. Thomas, 121
Gauger, Thomas, 40, 143, 151
Gelbloom, Gerald, 137
Genovese, Alfred, 33
Gericke, Wilhelm, 10–12, 61, 71, 90, 103–104, 107
Ghitalla, Armando, 56–57, 147, 148
Girard, Henri, 108
Glantz, Harry, 41
Glover, Ernest, 57
Goldovsky, Boris, 64
Gomberg, Harold, 54
Gomberg, Ralph, 2, 33, 54, 135, 138
Goodman, Saul, 57
Gordon, Peter, 41–42
Gray, Darlene, 33
Green, Reuben, 37, 148
Gustin, Daniel R., 25, 84, 85, 86

Hadcock, Peter, 148
Hale, Philip, 72
Hallberg, Gordon, 77, 120, 136, 146, 149
Hammerich, Richard, 124
Harper, James, 65
Hearne, Joseph, 136, 144, 147, 148
Hedberg, Earl, 111, 145, 149
Hendricks, Barbara, 75, 76
Henriot-Schweitzer, Nicole, 122
Henschel, Georg, 7, 8–10, 103, 107

Hidekazu, Yoshida, 119
Higginson, Henry Lee, 5–8, 10, 11, 13, 15–16, 81, 84–85, 94, 95–96, 97, 107, 155
Hobart, Max, 139, 141–142
Hobson, Ann, 34–35, 43, 143
Hoherman, Martin, 77
Hoseini, Shafi Al, 119
Howe, M, A. DeWolfe, 17, 61, 97, 104, 107
H.T.P., 17, 71–72
Humphrey, George, 148
Hwang, Bo Youp, 121, 145

Jeanneret, Marc, 15
Johnson, H. Earle, 72, 79, 80, 96
Judd, George E., 90, 96–98, 109, 130
Judson, Arthur, 97

Kadinoff, Bernard, 145
Kajimoto, Naoyasu, 125, 127
Kavalovski, Charles, 56
Kleinsinger, George, 47
Kneisel, Franz, 12
Knudsen, Ronald, 33, 34, 121, 134, 143
Kolb, Barbara, 115, 119
Koussevitsky, Serge, 15, 17, 18–19, 20, 29, 30, 31, 32, 37, 39, 40, 58, 61–62, 67, 68, 73, 80, 84, 97, 98, 107
Kraft, William, 152
Krupa, Gene, 40
Kuntz, Daniel, 109
Kupferberg, Herbert, 84
Kurland, Anita, 139

Langendoen, Jacopus, 109
Laurent, Georges, 38, 39, 43, 53
Laus, Abdon, 109
Lavelle, Paul, 57
Lefkowitz, Roman, 4, 33, 140, 146
Leginska, Ethel, 33
Leguia, Luis, 136, 146
Lehner, Eugene, 85
Leinsdorf, Erich, 20, 35, 49, 50, 64, 81, 131
Levenson, Sam, 142
Levy, Amnon, 145
Liegl, Ernst, 52
Lipson, Jerome, 36–38

Listemann, Bernhard, 7
Longy, Georges, 14

Maas, Louis, 7
McClane, Ralph, 54
Mackey, Richard, 121, 147, 148–149
Manos, Constantine, 154
Mariano, Joseph, 53
Marshall, William, 50
Martin, Leslie, 31, 39–40, 143
Marx, Harpo, 59
Mason, Redfern, 107
Matsumoto, Katsuo, 119
Mauricci, Vincent, 37
Mazzeo, Rosario, 81, 116–117
Melba, Nellie, 96
Messiaen, Olivier, 78
Miller, Glenn, 31, 32
Miller, Jonathan, 148
Mischakoff, Mischa, 41
Mitropoulos, Dmitri, 55
Miyagawa, Teruo, 127
Mizuno, Ikuko, 120–121
Moerschel, Joel, 145
Monteux, Pierre, 13–14, 15, 16–18, 58, 80, 96–97, 108
Morris, Mrs. Stephen V. C., 121
Morris, Thomas D., 91, 99
Morse, Elizabeth, 136
Moscovitz, Harry, 38
Moss, Leonard, 20, 124, 146
Moyer, Betsy, 136, 145, 148
Moyer, William, 21, 100, 136, 145, 148
Muck, Karl, 12, 13, 72, 79, 96, 105, 106
Munch, Charles, 3, 15, 20, 30, 32, 40, 46, 49, 53, 54, 57, 67, 70, 90, 97, 102, 108, 109, 110, 122

Nagy, Laszlo, 148
Nieland, Mischa, 137
Nikisch, Arthur, 12, 15, 79

Ohanian, David, 36, 143, 146, 147
Oliver, John, 66
Olson, Robert, 144
Oshima, Natsuko, 128
Ostrovsky, Fredy, 31–32

Ozawa, Seiji, 23, 74, 76, 84, 85, 91, 109, 115, 119, 122–123, 125, 127–128, 144

Pappoutsakis, James, 38–39, 116, 138
Paray, Paul, 31
Pares, Gabriel, 14
Partch, Harry, 40
Patterson, Jerome, 148
Paur, Emil, 12, 153
Perlman, Itzhak, 93
Perry, Thomas D., 15, 98–99, 101, 114, 138, 147, 153
Petrillo, James C., 18, 19, 98
Piatigorsky, Gregor, 50
Pierce, William, 92, 148
Pietropaolo, Joseph, 77, 136
Piller, Boaz, 13, 109
Plaster, Richard, 46, 120, 135, 148
Portnoi, Henry, 52, 134
Pottle, Ralph, 149, 150
Press, Arthur, 40, 143, 146, 151
Procter, Carol, 24, 33, 43, 77, 101, 116–117, 121, 144

Quinby, Winfield S., 90

Rabaud, Henri, 13–14, 80, 96–97
Rapier, Wayne, 69, 136
Reiner, Fritz, 44
Rhein, Will, 77
Ripley, Robert, 20, 32–33, 100
Robison, Alfred, 2, 64, 113–115
Rodzinski, Arthur, 32
Rose, Leonard, 50
Rosen, Jerome, 77, 147
Rotenberg, Sheldon, 37, 121, 146
Rubinstein, Anton, 7
Ruggiero, Matthew, 29–30, 136

Salkowski, John, 111, 144, 147
Salmond, Felix, 32
Sasson, Michel, 15, 142
Schaefer, Lois, 43, 144, 149
Schelling, Ernest, 139–140
Schmitz, Chester, 46–47
Schneider, Alfred, 134, 142, 145
Schub, André-Michel, 34, 136
Schuller, Gunther, 84, 85, 128

Schumann-Heink, Ernestine 96
Seigel, Harvey, 147
Sembrich, Marcella, 96
Sevitzky, Fabien, 36
Shanet, Howard, 140
Shapiro, Harry, 86, 95, 112
Shermont, Roger, 15
Shisler, William, 65
Silverstein, Joseph, 2, 33, 34, 48–50, 70, 74, 81, 84, 95, 140, 154
Sird, Raymond, 33, 134, 145
Skrowaczewski, Stanislaw, 46–47
Small, Roland, 35
Smedvig, Rolf, 33, 36, 143, 147
Smith, Charles, 57, 147, 152
Smith, Joanne, 152
Smith, Josephine, 152
Smith, Moses, 20
Sokoloff, Nikolai, 140–141
Speaker, Marylou, 25, 50, 139, 145, 147
Speyer, Louis, 14, 45, 46, 108–109
Starker, Janos, 51
Steinberg, Michael, 86
Steinberg, William, 77, 110
Still, Ray, 44
Stokowski, Leopold, 31, 54
Stone, George, 57
Svecenski, Louis, 12
Swallow, John, 35
Szulc, Roman, 57

Tabuteau, Marcel, 54, 55
Taft, Edward A., 121
Takechi, Mitsuru, 119
Tapley, Rolland, 141
Thomas, Michael Tilson, 73–74, 110
Thomas, Theodore, 5, 7, 104, 107
Thorstenberg, Laurence, 44–46, 47, 77–78, 120, 139
Toeplitz, Gideon, 94, 95, 112
Toscanini, Arturo, 19, 41

Uritsky, Vyacheslav, 15

Vacchiano, William, 56
Vared, Ilana, 126
Viscuglia, Felix, 40, 42, 143
Vitale, Michael, 136
Voisin, René, 87
Voisin, Roger, 87, 134
von Karajan, Herbert, 118, 140

Walt, Sherman, 55–56, 110, 147
Walter, Bruno, 53
Walter, W. E., 105, 106
Weems, Ted, 40
White, Lawrence, 57
Whitelaw, Jordan M., 90–92
Whiteman, Paul, 32
Wilfinger, Gottfried, 136–137
Wilkison, Ronald, 147
Winder, Max, 15
Wolfe, Lawrence, 140, 144
Woodworth, G. Wallace, 68
Wright, Harold ("Buddy"), 54–55, 70, 149
Wright, Ruth, 55, 149
Wuorinen, Charles, 73
Wurtzler, Bela, 30–31, 146

Yampolsky, Victor, 15, 50
Yancich, Charles, 33, 134

Zach, Max, 12
Zamkochian, Berj, 147
Zaretsky, Michael, 15
Zazofsky, George, 37, 134
Zazofsky, Peter, 134
Zeise, Karl, 145
Zerrahn, Carl, 5, 7
Zighéra, Alfred, 58
Zighéra, Bernard, 38–39, 58–59
Zukofsky, Paul, 73